In *Your Best Destiny*, Wintley Phipps takes the problematic portions of life and exposes them as opportunities to create positive outcomes in your own life and the lives of people around you. It is a wonderful tool to encourage everyone to lead a more productive life that contributes to society at large.

BENJAMIN S. CARSON SR., MD
Emeritus professor of neurosurgery, oncology, plastic surgery, and pediatrics, Johns Hopkins Medicine; president and CEO of American Business Collaborative, LLC

What a wonderful service Wintley Phipps has rendered by reminding us that anyone can experience success God's way. If you plan to read only one book on success this year, I enthusiastically recommend *Your Best Destiny*.

BARRY C. BLACK
Chaplain of the United States Senate

Reading *Your Best Destiny* is a warming, encouraging, and enriching experience. It is in the heart and soul of our being, in the depths of our respective journeys, that we find strength and insight into what it truly means to love, hope, and abundantly live as we trust God with who we are created to be. This book awakens in the reader an understanding of the source of grace and abounding joy!

LT. COLONEL KENNETH W. MAYNOR
Salvation Army Territorial Program Secretary, USA Eastern Territory

Wintley Phipps has crafted a moving book of eloquence, insight, and biblical wisdom. It comes as a gift. This is a book to read and to share—never more needed than now.

KEVIN BELMONTE
Lead script consultant for the film *Amazing Grace* and author of *D. L. Moody: A Life*

Decisions create destinies, and Wintley's book will help you make wise decisions. His passion to help you reach your highest and best will take you through a journey of eight key pillars that will greatly aid you in navigating the challenge of making solid and wise decisions in today's constantly changing world. So pick it up, find a quiet place, and launch an adventure you'll be glad that you took time to have.

DR. BOB RECCORD
President/CEO, Hope for the Heart

Your Best Destiny is a must-read for all who seek to excel and achieve in life. Wintley illustrates that goals and achievements in life are important; but without empathy in the fullest sense of the word, we all fall short. Insightful and creative, *Your Best Destiny* will challenge you to protect the greatest piece of real estate you own—the six inches between your ears.

JODY VICTOR
Public speaker and Amway Crown Independent Business Owner

Wintley's friendship, wisdom, and discernment have steered me through many a dark season in this crucible of life, illuminating the countless treasures the Lord had hidden along the way—treasures I otherwise could have missed. His profound insight into God's character makes him the perfect companion for a journey toward understanding why each of us is here on this earth. *Your Best Destiny* is an inspiring yet practical guide to seeing yourself as God sees you and discovering with confidence the unique path He's called you to walk. As Wintley writes, "The best version of ourselves that we can be . . . is not about what we *do* . . . but about *who we are* at the core." These words flow not just from Wintley's pen but also from his heart, for *who he is* truly embodies the principles and guidance that he shares.

MATT CROUCH
President of Trinity Broadcasting Network

Your Best Destiny is a life-changing book, destined to become a classic that will enable Christians and non-Christians alike to grasp a new vision of the life that God meant for each of us to live. Both visionary and immensely practical, it is one of the clearest, most insightful, and most engaging books on the steps to spiritual growth. Full of wisdom, optimism, and grace, it is a wake-up call from business-as-usual for contemporary Christians. It calls for a radical redefinition of what it really means to be a Christian in today's society, and it presents—in novel, compelling, and memorable ways—an in-depth but clear blueprint of timeless truths about finding one's true purpose in life. It is a must-read for anyone and everyone who wants to delve beneath the superficial and truly discover—with tested tools—what it takes to live a life that makes a lasting difference in the world.

DAVID R. WILLIAMS, PHD
Florence and Laura Norman Professor of Public Health, Harvard School of Public Health; professor of African and African American Studies, Harvard University

I've known Wintley Phipps for many years, and his is a story of small beginnings. He was born and raised on the island of Trinidad with nothing but a dream and a prayer. Yet God has used him to impact the lives of millions of people around the world, including kings, queens, and presidents. This book is for those who want to become the person they were created to be. Many Christians spend a great portion of their lives searching for answers to the question, "What is God's plan for my life?" If you are one of these people, you don't have to wait any longer. If you feel like your life is floundering or you are in a "rut" with no way out, then this book is for you. Wintley beautifully and methodically outlines the major principles set forth in Scripture to help you to realize your best destiny.

DANNY SHELTON
Founder, Three Angels Broadcasting Network

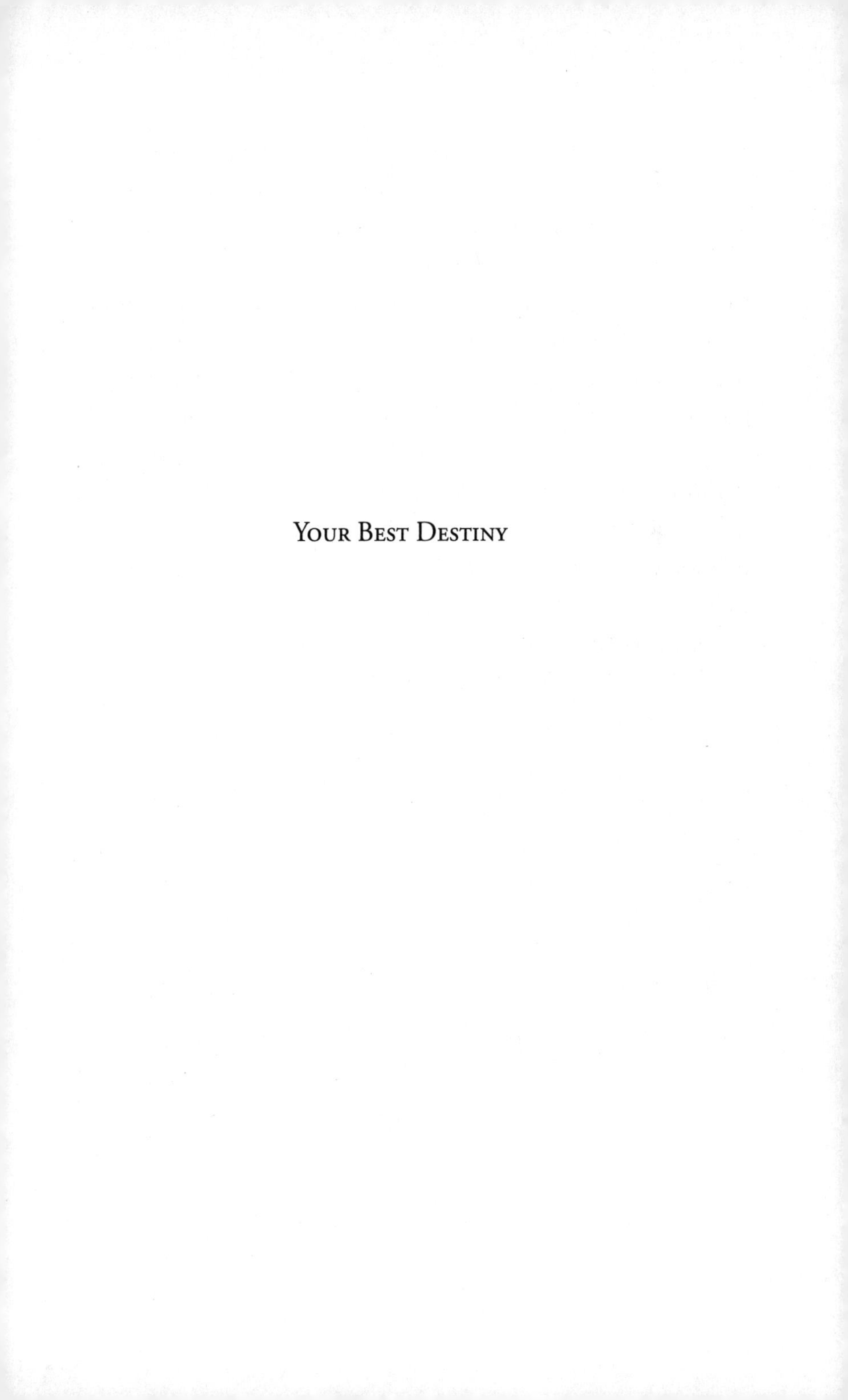

Your Best Destiny

YOUR *best* DESTINY

Becoming the person you were created to be

WINTLEY PHIPPS

with James Lund

An Imprint of
Tyndale House Publishers, Inc.

Visit Tyndale Momentum online at www.tyndalemomentum.com.

TYNDALE, Tyndale Momentum, and the Tyndale Momentum logo are registered trademarks of Tyndale House Publishers, Inc.

Your Best Destiny: Becoming the Person You Were Created to Be

Edited by Karin Stock Buursma

Designed by Mark Anthony Lane II

Published in association with the literary agency of WordServe Literary Group, www.wordserve literary.com.

Library of Congress Cataloging-in-Publication Data

Phipps, Wintley.
Your best destiny: becoming the person you were created to be / Wintley Phipps with James Lund.
pages cm
Includes bibliographical references.
ISBN 978-1-4964-0794-8 (hc) — ISBN 978-1-4143-90307 (sc)
1. Phipps, Wintley. 2. Gospel musicians—United States—Biography. 3. Christian biography—United States. I. Lund, James L. II. Title.
ML420.P496A3 2015
248.4—dc23 2015008680

SC (ITPE) 978-1-4964-1198-3

Printed in the United States of America

21 20 19 18 17 16 15
7 6 5 4 3 2 1

To my wife, Linda, and my three sons, Wintley II, Winston, and Wade. Your love and support have contributed immeasurably to all of the greatest blessings and accomplishments in my life. Building and nurturing a family has been one of my greatest joys and privileges and has shaped and strengthened me in ways I could only have dreamed of.

Contents

Acknowledgments

Someone once said that love may be silent but gratitude must speak. Allow me to express my gratitude to all those who have helped me on this literary journey. This book has been years in the making and has become a reality because of some gifted people and kind encouragers. Thank you to Rebecca, Cliff, and Melanie; Greg and Alice at WordServe Literary; Jan and Sharon at Tyndale Momentum; and all who are part of my new Tyndale family. A very special thanks to James Lund, my colleague, collaborator, and friend. To my sister Oprah, who kept asking, "Where's the book?" Well, it's finally here.

To my sons, Wintley II, Winston, and Wade. I will continue to pray that the life I live before you so resembles, reflects, and reveals the character of Christ that it inspires you to fall more in love with Jesus every day.

To my wife, Linda, who has taught me more about the character of God than any human being I know. Thank you for being so tender and so strong, so courageous and so beautiful, inside and out. My prayer is that through our marriage you will taste a little bit of heaven on earth and that God will smile on you through me.

A book of this kind challenges us, as imperfect vessels, to so live that our conduct will always rise to the level of the principles we articulate. All of us will often have to fall at the feet of Jesus and weep over our mistakes. May we ever remember that God's best life for us, should we live it, is really His life living in us.

> My old self has been crucified with Christ. It is no longer I who live, but Christ lives in me. So I live in this earthly body by trusting in the Son of God, who loved me and gave himself for me.
>
> GALATIANS 2:20

Introduction

It is no accident that you picked up this book. You're searching for something.

Perhaps you sense that your life is off-kilter. Maybe you've just noticed it, or maybe you've lived with a feeling of frustration for years. Perhaps you just closed a chapter in your life and aren't sure where to turn next. Whatever led you to this point, though, you now realize that you're not moving. You're not growing. You're unsatisfied and seeking more—but more *what*?

My hunch is that you're after something rewarding. Something transforming. Something lasting. Something that blows away old definitions of success and replaces them with truth you feel at the center of your soul.

That "something" you seek is God's best life for you. It is what you dream about in the corners of your imagination. It is everything good and right for you and your future. It is what I call your best destiny, and it means being the best *you* that you can possibly be. Your destiny is within your reach if you are willing to risk a few steps into the unknown.

How can I—a pastor, gospel singer, and family man—make

this bold promise? Because my solution for your life does not originate with me. It is based on timeless truths, on wisdom that has guided men and women since their beginnings. It comes from God.

Now, when it comes to God, I don't know where you stand. It could be you're a longtime believer who is feeling stuck in your spiritual life. Or maybe you've just entered into a relationship with Him and are looking to deepen your faith. Perhaps you are still in the process of defining your belief.

Wherever you are on the journey of faith, I invite you to take another step. No matter what you believe, you'll find material here that can help you. What I'm about to reveal can lead you to real, God-defined success. We're going to explore eight secrets that will enable you to discover who you are at the core of your being, and help you to frame a vision for the best destiny you could ever achieve. They will show you how to strip away the burden of beliefs and behaviors that hinder your every move so that God can refashion you into the person you were born to be. When you finally discard the crusty exterior of your old life and take the form you were created for, you will unveil greatness—a greatness you never knew was possible.

I have met some of the world's best-known people and studied their lives. They include Billy Graham, Mother Teresa, Nelson Mandela, and Oprah Winfrey, as well as the last six American presidents. I've also met and observed people just as extraordinary whose feet will never walk the red carpet and whose faces will never appear on the cover of *Time* magazine. I could make the case that each of these people, whether famous or anonymous, has lived aspects of God's best life for them—a life that reflects greatness.

But what exactly does it mean to be great? We'll soon see that greatness has nothing to do with wealth, power, position, or fame, though these can be by-products of great living. Everything I have experienced as a person of faith, a professional vocal artist, a pastor, a founder of a nonprofit education program, a husband and father, and a man has shown me that greatness is not what we *do* but who we *are*—and its rewards are rich indeed:

- Confidence
- Hope
- Fulfillment
- Impact
- Peace
- A sense of purpose
- Joy

This book is designed to bring your life into clear focus and to open your eyes to your amazing potential as an extraordinary individual. It will summon you to greatness and show you your role in bringing God's best life to the world.

You won't be alone in this venture. To help you along, an interactive online experience will connect you with a community of encouraging, like-minded people who are on the same journey of self-exploration. Look in the back pages of this book for directions on where to find your *complimentary assessment code* so you can access the Your Best Destiny Personal Assessment Tool.

Each chapter includes study questions that you can answer on your own or discuss with your home group, Bible study, Sunday-school class, or friends over coffee. While you'll find that the concepts in this book apply to you as a unique individual, they also work well in a group with joint accountability and focus. I encourage you to read this book with others. A shared journey increases motivation and camaraderie and can often lead to fresh insights.

Do you want to discover your God-given destiny—the life you were born to live? So do I. Let's step into it together.

Finding the Best *You*

By the time you've read this book, you will understand the importance of eight essential ethical "pillars" that will support your growth as you seek to become the best *you* that you can be.

After years of research, and with the help of Dr. William Sedlacek—professor emeritus of education at the University of Maryland and one of the nation's leading authorities on noncognitive assessment—my team and I have identified more than one hundred dimensions of God's character. From this list, we created a comprehensive questionnaire, the Your Best Destiny Personal Assessment Tool, that will help you identify your strengths and what you can do to develop a godly character. You will find this practical assessment tool in the appendix at the end of the book.

I encourage you to answer the questions and then go to our website—www.YourBestDestinyAssessment.com. From your answers, you'll receive feedback on where your strengths lie and where you might need to focus your attention to further develop your character. This assessment may be used individually or with a group.

Our website is also filled with resources based on the chapter themes in this book: questions, sermons, music, books, encouragement, and insight tailored to your individual needs. All of these resources are designed to help you assess, diagnose, prescribe, and implement. They will help to transform you from the inside out. They will empower you, with God's help, to *resemble*, *reflect*, and *reveal* His character. When you do that, everything becomes possible.

Are you ready to move out of the mundane, pursue your destiny, and become the best *you* that you can possibly be? Let's get started.

1

DISCOVERING YOUR BEST DESTINY

How to Uncover God's Best Life for You

Every person's life is a fairy tale written by God's fingers.

HANS CHRISTIAN ANDERSEN

On a four-lane highway, a traffic light changed from red to green. Like an eager racehorse bursting from the gate, a sleek red Chevrolet surged forward. One by one, the other vehicles on the road fell behind. Only a silver Lincoln presented any challenge to the speeding red streak that turned night into day with its powerful headlights. Soon the Lincoln faded into the background as well.

The Chevrolet ate up the miles as the motor throbbed and the driver's hands tightened on the steering wheel. A triumphant smile curved his lips. His dark eyes gleamed with delight. There wasn't an auto on the highway that could keep up with his. There also wasn't a better driver, not in the whole United States.

A warning sign signaled a bend in the road. The driver braked, his body leaning right as the huge car banked around the steep bend. A glance in the rearview mirror showed a pair of headlights gaining on him. The driver's eyes narrowed. His foot pressed harder on the gas pedal. The driver watched his speeding car's quivering needle climb to eighty . . . ninety . . . one hundred miles per hour. He would push his mechanical monster as fast and far as it could go. No one would catch him. The driver released a low, exultant chuckle. *This* was living.

Suddenly a voice cut through the sound of the roaring engine and the driver's sense of satisfaction.

"Wintley? You come on in now. Time for supper."

The vision of the daring driver and the powerful Chevrolet vanished faster than a speeding race car at the Indianapolis 500. In the vision's place sat its creator—an imaginative, curly-haired five-year-old gripping a red tricycle.

That young "speed demon" was me.

I have always been a dreamer. As a boy growing up on the island of Trinidad, I often turned my dented and rusted red tricycle into a magic carpet. I flipped the trike on its side, gripped a back tire as if it were a steering wheel, and imagined myself controlling a fancy car or powerful transport truck. At other times I pictured myself wearing a leather helmet, gloves, and thick-lensed goggles as I peered at the instrument panel and directed my open-cockpit plane up, up into an azure sky.

Today, I live a short drive from Orlando, Florida—the home of Disney World, a place that cultivates and embellishes youthful dreams. Whether it's returning to a land of magic kingdoms and fairy tales or of pirates and space rangers, we enjoy revisiting the fantasies of our youth.

Can you remember your childhood dreams? Did you imagine yourself as a soldier, sailor, cowboy, fireman, or policeman? Were you a princess, pilot, dancer, or animal trainer? Do you ever think about those dreams today?

Some people dismiss childhood hopes and dreams as silly delusions, unrealistic whims that are best buried and forgotten. I would argue, however, that they are more than just animated flights of fancy. They signal our beginning awareness of an amazing potential future that stretches beyond what we can now see or hear.

They are our first yearnings for our God-given destiny.

Something about those words should stir a shiver of excitement inside us. They connect us to long-lost visions, to the belief that a significant future awaits us.

Our dreams tend to mature and change as we grow older. We learn more about ourselves and our gifts. If we're fortunate, we develop our abilities and passions and discover new possibilities. Dreams give us the inspiration to keep pursuing our best selves.

A man once uttered these words at a speech contest in Atlanta:

> We cannot have an enlightened democracy with one great group living in ignorance. We cannot have a healthy nation with one-tenth of the people ill-nourished, sick, harboring germs of disease which recognize no color lines—obey no Jim Crow laws. We cannot have a nation orderly and sound with one group so ground down and thwarted that it is almost forced into unsocial attitudes and crime. We cannot be truly Christian people so long as we flout the central teachings of Jesus: brotherly love and the Golden Rule. We cannot come to full prosperity with one great group so ill-delayed that it cannot buy goods. So as we gird ourselves to defend democracy from foreign

> attack, let us see to it that increasingly at home we give fair play and free opportunity for all people.[1]

The speaker won the contest. You may recognize the eloquence, the passion, and the cause for which the speaker fought. You may also know his name: Dr. Martin Luther King Jr. What you may not know, however, is that, at the time of this speech, he wasn't yet Dr. King. He was a teenager, fifteen years old. Even at that young age, he was hearing the call toward his destiny. He was already moving into God's best life for him.

Maybe you know folks who have always understood what they were supposed to do with their lives. The door to their ideal future opened at just the right time and they sauntered on through. For the rare few, the road to fulfilling their hopes is marked by brightly lit traffic signs with giant letters: "NEXT EXIT: YOUR DESTINY."

For most of us, however, that's not how it works.

If you're anything like me, you've struggled to find your place and purpose in life. You have gone to school, studied books, observed the lives of others, sought wise counsel, and gained practical experience. More than once, you have embarked on a promising trail only to reach a dead end. You've searched and strained, yet God's best life for you has proven elusive.

How do you know? Because you sense it in your soul. You go through each day feeling unfulfilled. Deep down, you're sure you have untapped potential. You live with a nagging impression that you were made for more than this. And when that frustration persists over time, month after month and year after year, it infects your work, your relationships, and your faith. You begin to grow fatigued. Disheartened. Cynical.

Disillusioned.

I understand the feeling because I've known it myself.

Is This All There Is?

When I was ten, my family and I moved from our tropical home on the small island of Trinidad to the frigid big city: Montreal in Quebec, Canada. The dramatic change in environment opened my eyes to the world. I discovered that I had a talent for singing, and I saw myself flying around the globe, performing in front of thousands of adoring fans. That, I was sure, would be God's best life for me.

I found a crack in my picture of the best life, however, on the day I posed as a reporter and sneaked into the Montreal Forum. It was 1970, I was fifteen years old, and I was prepared to do just about anything to see Sly and the Family Stone perform. (Yes, I am that old, and yes, I had a lot of nerve back then.) At the time, Sylvester Stewart, better known as Sly Stone, was at the top of the music scene. He was a pioneer of funk and soul music. He'd appeared the summer before at the legendary Woodstock festival, and his band's latest single, "Thank You (Falettinme Be Mice Elf Agin)," was number one on the charts. Sly was one of my idols—that is, until the night of the concert.

Before the show, I was backstage with two cameras around my neck, doing my best impression of a newsman who actually belonged there. I was listening to the crowd chant "Sly-y . . . Sly-y . . ." when a limousine pulled up. My jaw dropped when Sly's handlers lifted out a frail, disoriented heap of a man and almost carried him into his dressing room. From there, they hustled the rock star into a shower stall and turned the water on him. Within seconds he was drenched and screaming as if possessed.

I was stunned. This was a rock star? This was my hero? Later I read about Sly's drug issues and conflicts with other members of the band. He was not a happy man.

I'd always assumed that money, influence, and adulation ensured a successful life. Now I wasn't so certain.

Have you had the same thought—that true greatness lies in acquiring wealth, power, fame, or the adoration of others? Most of us believe this at some level, even if it's subconscious. Whether or not we realize it, we shape our thinking, behavior, and careers by this belief. We say to ourselves, "When I earn that manager's job and the salary that goes with it, then I'll have it made," or, "If more people at my office, in my neighborhood, or at my church knew me and recognized my abilities, then I'd be happy with my life." So we keep pushing ourselves for that promotion and keep trying to amaze people who pay us little attention.

I've noticed something, though, about those of us who behave this way. Even if we eventually achieve our goal of riches or renown, we often find that it leaves us disappointed and disoriented, dissatisfied with our place in the world.

John D. Rockefeller founded Standard Oil Company and became the wealthiest man in the world. "I have made many millions," he said, "but they have brought me no happiness."[2] Henry Ford, founder and president of Ford Motor Company, once said, "I was happier when doing a mechanic's job."[3]

"The rich are never happy, no matter what they have," explains author Robert Frank. "There was this man who owned a 100-foot yacht. I said: 'This is a terrific boat.' He said: 'Look down the harbor.' We looked down the marina, and there were boats two and three times as large. He said, 'My 100-foot yacht today is like a dinghy compared to these other boats.'"[4]

Psychoanalyst Manfred Kets de Vries explains the problem this way: "For the super-rich, houses, yachts, cars, and planes are like new toys that they play with for five minutes and then lose interest in. Pretty soon, to attain the same buzz they have to spend more money. All the spending is a mad attempt to cover up boredom and depression."[5]

Boredom and depression—hardly hallmarks of a successful life. Contrary to popular belief, money does not buy happiness; neither does power, popularity, or adoration. Maybe you've heard of an old country song, "Lookin' for Love (in All the Wrong Places)"? That is what so many of us do—look for God's best life for us in all the wrong ways and all the wrong places.

Our twisted definitions of success can be even more destructive when applied to our view of God.

Think about this. If you have any kind of faith in a God who is responsible for your existence—and if you believe in your heart (whether you admit it or not) that He has created you for the purpose of amassing fortune, influence, fame, and the adulation of others—then what kind of God is He? What does that mean for your faith? How is that external, achievement-centered spirituality going to express itself in your life?

I'll tell you. You will become more and more disappointed in God if He doesn't give you what you think you deserve. Your increased cynicism may lead you to fall away from faith altogether, thinking that it's not worth it if it doesn't benefit you in tangible ways. Or if you remain part of a church, you may find yourself detached, singing the same songs and praying the same prayers and feeling bored by the routine. You may try to lead others to your faith just to add another notch in your evangelistic belt, or you may attend a church that's more concerned with adding members than with teaching what you need to know. You may read your Bible and other Christian books and follow their rules, yet feel disconnected from God. You may have learned to pretend, to tell people who ask that "everything is fine," when in fact your faith is in crisis.

You will ask yourself, *Is this God's best life for me? Is this all there is?*

The answer to both questions is *no*. There is more. But to discover it, you may have to dramatically adjust your thinking.

Is God Trying to Tell You Something?

My thinking was anything but clear after my Montreal encounter with Sly Stone. I was confused. Yet I remained convinced that my future was in show business. I still had big dreams for myself. I was ready to advance my singing career any way I could. When a man approached me about the idea of performing at a Montreal nightclub, the Penthouse Two, I jumped at the chance. Soon a friend and I were headlining there.

It was during this time that I almost destroyed my dreams. I'd seen one of the stars of rock and roll, Little Richard, put on an incredible performance at a concert in Montreal. I decided I needed to sound more like him, so I did my own screaming rendition of two of his songs at a school talent show. The crowd loved it, but when I woke up the next morning I could barely speak, let alone sing. A doctor said I'd damaged my throat and voice box. There was no guarantee I would recover. Fortunately, after I didn't speak for a week, my singing ability returned—but my screaming days were over.

Sometimes it takes a near disaster for God to get our attention. That was certainly the case for me. It dawned on me after the screaming episode that God might be trying to tell me something.

When I was very young, my father wasn't active in any church. My mother, however, was serious about her Christian faith, and she passed that on to her sons. As far back as I can remember, she took my younger brother, Wendell, and me to church every week.

I'd always believed in God. He'd always been part of my life. I understood, at least to some degree, that He loved me and had created everything in the universe, including me.

I allowed God and His wisdom to guide me—most of the time. But I hadn't surrendered to Him completely. I hadn't yet embraced the biblical idea that "everything got started in him and finds its purpose in him."[6] I wasn't ready to trust my future to Him. I was still firmly in charge of my life.

Maybe you can relate. Perhaps you believe in God and His power over your world. Perhaps you have faith that He loves you. But maybe you're also holding something back. Maybe you, too, have your own plan for achieving your best destiny, and you aren't sure if God is on the same page.

God's plans were increasingly on my mind after my failed attempt at becoming the next Little Richard. I wondered whether God was speaking to me. I'd been given a glimpse of the dark side of fame and been discouraged from adopting a rock-and-roll style. Was this more than coincidence? Maybe show business—at least the kind I was pursuing—wasn't the path to God's best life for me. I decided to give up my nightclub dreams and promised God that from then on I would sing only songs that helped people spiritually.

Is God trying to tell *you* something? Has He closed doors or discouraged you from a path you desperately want to follow? Is that what led you to this book? Are you sensing that His picture of success is different from yours?

What I needed to realize back then, and what God may be telling you now, is that His view of things—including success—is not at all like ours. In fact, it may be the opposite. The Bible says, "You are always making yourselves look good, but God sees what is in your heart. The things that most people think are important are worthless as far as God is concerned."[7]

We like to "look good"—but appearances can deceive, can't they? A sports car for sale may shine from a fresh wash, but under the hood, its engine needs a complete overhaul. A house may present a beautiful yard and exterior, but inside its walls, termites are on the attack. An apple may look tasty on the outside yet be tainted on the inside.

Does this matter to us? Of course! No one wants a car ready to break down, a home infested with bugs, or a rotten apple. Yet when it comes to people, our attitude often seems to indicate the opposite. We act as if what's inside isn't important. We cheer for the superstar athlete and ignore his extramarital affairs. We fawn over the movie actress who regularly makes outrageous and untrue statements about others. We try to win the support of the business owner who won his or her wealth through shady deals.

Why do we admire these people? Why do we strive to be more like them? It's because, from our vantage point, it *appears* they're living God's best life for them. We see the money and celebrity and wish we were in their shoes. What we don't see, however, is that some of these people are tainted on the inside. Behind the glitz and glamour designed to impress us are pain, personal struggle, and poor choices.

Isn't our plan for a fulfilled life also made up of things that will impress people, whether that's money and the objects it buys, a job with a fancy title, or talent that earns the adulation of fans? God sees right through us. He knows we're trying to make ourselves look good so we can think of ourselves as successful. And He says these things are worthless.

But if all this is worthless, what *is* success? What is God's best life for us?

BECOMING YOUR BEST YOU

What dreams for your life did you have as a child? What dreams do you still have today?

What comes to mind when you think of a successful life? How much are money, fame, and power tied up with your definition of success?

Do you believe at some level that God has created you for the purpose of amassing fortune, influence, or fame? If so, what does that say about Him and what He is like?

What do you think it means to be the best *you* that you can be?

Dear God, You know the dreams I have for my life and my longing for something more. And You also know that some of the things I long for will just leave me feeling empty. Help me to consider Your definition of success as I begin to learn about the best life You have for me. Amen.

2

YOU ARE A MASTERPIECE

How to Identify True Success

Watch your thoughts, they become words;
watch your words, they become actions;
watch your actions, they become habits;
watch your habits, they become character;
watch your character, for it becomes your destiny.

FRANK OUTLAW

Meryl Streep is one of the most respected actresses of our time. She has won three Academy Awards and eight Golden Globe awards and has been nominated for more major acting awards than anyone else in Hollywood. Her take on success? "You don't have to be famous," she once said during a college commencement address. "You just have to make your mother and father proud of you."[1]

Barack Obama, a former state and US senator, is the forty-fourth president of the United States and the first African-American to hold the office. During another commencement address he said, "I've come to affirm that one's title, even a title like President of the United States, says very little about how well one's life has been led."[2]

Walter Cronkite, a journalism icon and anchor of *CBS Evening News* for nearly twenty years, was known as "the most trusted man in America." He once said, "Success is more permanent when you achieve it without destroying your principles."[3]

Through nonviolent civil disobedience, Mahatma Gandhi led his native India to independence and inspired movements for civil rights and freedom around the world. He said, "As human beings, our greatness lies not so much in being able to remake the world—that is the myth of the atomic age—as in being able to remake ourselves."[4]

Each of these famous people has recorded amazing accomplishments. Each has lived what most would describe as a commendable life. Yet each also seems to feel that success involves more than doing great things.

They are on to something. There is more to successful living than what can be listed on a résumé or measured in a bank account. And despite what the media implies, God's best life for us doesn't arrive when we buy the right shampoo, sunglasses, or smart phone. If we honestly want a genuine, life-altering definition of success, we shouldn't expect to find it in a TV commercial. We need to look deeper—*soul* deep.

I am saying that the source of true success is not secular, but spiritual. As I learned many years ago, if we want to understand God's best life for us and what it means to find our best destiny, we must listen to God.

Back in Canada, after I nearly destroyed my voice and decided to walk away from a career as a rock singer, most of my public appearances involved singing at churches. One of these performances, at a church in Toronto, was attended by the head of the music department at a small school in Ontario: Kingsway College. Soon afterward, I received a scholarship offer to go to school there.

It seemed that God was opening an important door for me, but I planned to walk through it on my own terms.

I arrived in Oshawa, Ontario, sporting an afro and wearing platform shoes and a dashiki. You could say that I didn't exactly blend in at Kingsway. I enjoyed the music part and could handle the classes, but the rest of life at the school really got under my skin. Spartan meals, served only at certain times of the day. No leaving campus without permission. Lights out at 10 p.m. No holding hands with girls.

For a young man used to being his own boss, it was too much. I certainly did not believe that this was a fulfilled life.

One Friday night I was late for supper and found the cafeteria closed. I was hungry and furious. I went to the dean of men and told him I'd had enough of Kingsway. I was leaving as soon as I could get a train out of town. I said, "We're not allowed to do anything that we want to do."

For a long moment, the dean did not speak. Then he looked me in the eye. "Wintley," he said, "why don't you, for once, do not what *you* want to do but what *God* wants you to do?"

The dean's blunt response hit me like a ten-ton truck. I was thinking hard while I walked away from our meeting. As I climbed the dimly lit stairs to my room, my heart strained under a load of conviction. I realized that I would never be fulfilled, have peace, or know success until I yielded to God's irresistible will. I had to trust in *His* definition of the best life for me.

I was finally beginning to discover what it meant to pursue *God's* best life for me.

My father, by this time a practicing Christian, had actually given me a hint two years earlier. A talent scout had heard me sing and invited me to attend an exclusive high school in an affluent Montreal neighborhood. I wasn't sure that I wanted to accept.

"Go on, Wintley," my dad urged. "You attend school there. It's a great privilege." Dad wasn't one for wearing his heart on his sleeve or making speeches, but I could see that he was proud I had the opportunity to attend such a well-known school.

"They won't sing my kind of music," I said in a sullen voice. The truth was that I wasn't sure I wanted to go to a school where I would be the one brown face among hundreds of white ones. "I'll stick out like a sore thumb."

My dad's wise words came to mean even more to me as the years passed. "Don't worry about that," he said. "It's what's inside that counts."

All my life, I'd been focused on what I would *do* to be successful. My dreams were all about the places I would go and the achievements I would attain. Through a simple but profound truth, however, my father showed me another perspective, one that sets our usual thinking on its head. It's what our Father in heaven wants us all to learn: Our success in life is defined *from the inside out* rather than from the outside in. Money, titles, achievements, and recognition don't mean a thing if we're empty on the inside. Success is defined not in terms of the flesh but in terms of the spirit.

The Bible says, "People judge by outward appearance, but the LORD looks at the heart."[5] God's best life for us—that is, being the best version of ourselves that we can be—is not about what we *do* or how we appear to others, but *who we are* at the core.

Squeezed like a Sponge

The word *ethos,* originally from the Greek language, describes our customs, habits, and morals. It is the source of the English word *ethics*. Our ethos is a combination of our personality, character, emotions, guiding beliefs, habits, ideals, attitudes, fundamental values, and lifestyle. It is the moral home in which we dwell, the moral covers under which we sleep.

We often go to great lengths to disguise what's inside us. We might be sick or desperately worried about losing our job, but when someone asks how we're doing, we say, "Fine." When we strip away the masks and cover-ups, however, what remains is our ethos. It is who we are, our unique soul fingerprint, our truest self. It is what helps shape our destiny.

It is the compass that points us toward—or away from—God's best life for us.

The first step to achieving our goal, then, is to fully understand our ethos. How can we do that? Let's imagine for a moment that you've been washing the sink or the car with a sponge. Now it's time to clean up. You need to give that sponge a good squeeze. When you do, everything comes out—the good stuff, like the soap and water, and the bad stuff, like the dirt and grime.

Your ethos is a lot like a sponge. When you squeeze it—that is, put it under intense pressure—what emerges is your true ethos, both the good and the bad.

Jesus could have been talking about ethos when He told His disciples, "It's what comes out of a person that pollutes: obscenities, lusts, thefts, murders, adulteries, greed, depravity, deceptive dealings, carousing, mean looks, slander, arrogance, foolishness—all these are vomit from the heart. *There* is the source of your pollution."[6]

Another time, Jesus said, "A good person produces good things from the treasury of a good heart, and an evil person produces evil things from the treasury of an evil heart. What you say flows from what is in your heart."[7]

It's another way of saying what my father told me: It's what is inside that counts. Some people produce pollution; others enhance and encourage. Ultimately, it is men and women of exceptional character who inspire us. These are the people who are truly satisfied and fulfilled. These are the people who have discovered their God-given destiny.

You and I are under pressure every day, and so every day we have the opportunity to observe our ethos. We're driving down the freeway and another motorist cuts us off. We're barely making ends meet and the stranger walking ahead of us accidentally drops his wallet. During a school conference, a teacher makes a cutting comment about one of our kids.

How about it? How do *you* respond when the pressure is on?

Jim Daly, president of Focus on the Family, tells the story of how one father responded when a simple walk to McDonald's with his four-year-old daughter turned deadly:

> This father noticed that a car coming their way was moving erratically. The vehicle suddenly roared in their direction—and there was no time to escape. The surrounding buildings were built nearly on top of the sidewalks, so there was nowhere to run. Just before impact, the father grabbed his daughter and held her above his head.
>
> She lived. He died.[8]

Are you anything like this father—so filled with love that you would give your life in an instant? Do you possess qualities that vomit out pollution or that put you on a path to God's best life for you? What is your character? Who are you at the core?

Maybe you're a little afraid to answer those questions. Perhaps you fear what you'll find if you look too closely. Maybe you even feel the need to escape your ethos. Perhaps that's what you've been doing for years—chasing superficial visions of success, pretending that everything is fine while knowing deep down that something is rotten at the core.

If so, I have good news for you. Your ethos can change. If you're not happy with what you see inside of yourself—if you feel about as far from God's best life as a person can be—there *is* hope. You were created and intended for something far different than what you are currently experiencing.

The catch is that you can't change your ethos all on your own. You must put yourself in the hands of the Master Artist.

Modeled after God

In 1496, a twenty-one-year-old sculptor visited Rome for the first time. His arrival there coincided with an exhibition of recently unearthed works of classical art that celebrated moral virtue, physical beauty, and truth. Soon the young sculptor was engaged in a work of his own, one that would connect the ideals of an earlier era to the naturalist views of his day. The project would seal his reputation as the greatest sculptor of his time and perhaps of any period.

The sculptor, Michelangelo, carved his famous *Pietà* out of marble. Nearly six feet tall and more than six feet wide, it features the Virgin Mary cradling the body of her crucified son, Jesus, in her lap. Mary is portrayed as youthful and pure, wearing magnificent robes that flow to the ground. Jesus is at peace, graceful in death. It is a stunning sculpture.

To guide himself as he worked, Michelangelo typically created a smaller version of his intended project, made of terra-cotta, wax, or both. He possessed a photographic memory and was an excellent judge of proportion. Employing a drill, chisel, and files while working on the *Pietà*, he achieved an incredibly fine sheen and unprecedented detail and grandeur. When completed in 1499, the *Pietà* was hailed as one of the world's great masterpieces, and today it is considered by many as Michelangelo's most exceptional work.

Somehow, Michelangelo was able to look at a block of stone and, with only his tools and imagination, chip away the rough and unyielding exterior until he produced a result for the ages. He was so expert at his craft that many referred to him as "the divine one."

There is, however, an artist even greater and more truly divine than Michelangelo. His works of art are sculpted not out of stone but out of bones and skin. You and I are His masterpieces. And when it was time to decide on a model for His creations, He chose Himself:

> So God created human beings in his own image. In the image of God he created them; male and female he created them.[9]

Stop and let this fact sink in. The God of the universe designed *you* to resemble . . . *Him*. Not your Uncle Billy or Aunt Bertha. Not the family war hero from generations ago. God Himself.

Because God is spirit and not flesh, He did not create us with a physical resemblance in mind. His intention was everything else: the character, beliefs, values, and attitudes that make you the unique person you are yet also establish you in the image of God. He created you with an ethos modeled after His own. One that would lead you to the life He intended for you from the beginning.

I can hear your question already: "So what happened? My life feels more like a jigsaw puzzle where the pieces don't fit than a work of art designed by God!"

I'll tell you what happened. You've been battered by the sickness and struggle of this imperfect world. Beaten down by frustrations and failures. Broken by the loss of loved ones. You've sought success and watched it slip from your grasp. In that process of struggling, striving, and falling short, your shape has changed. You no longer reflect God's image as clearly. You more closely resemble an unformed lump of clay.

Yet in the hands of a great artist, even a lump like you or me can be transformed into something beautiful. That's what the prophet Jeremiah discovered many years ago:

> The LORD gave another message to [me]. He said, "Go down to the potter's shop, and I will speak to you there." So I did as he told me and found the potter working at his wheel. But the jar he was making did not turn out as he had hoped, so he crushed it into a lump of clay again and started over.
>
> Then the LORD gave me this message: "O Israel, can I not do to you as this potter has done to his clay? As the clay is in the potter's hand, so are you in my hand."[10]

God is ready to make a fresh start with you. He is eager to refashion you into the masterpiece He imagined when He first created you, one that reflects His glory and enables you to experience your God-given destiny. It can happen if you yield to the work and will of God in eight specific areas.

The Eight Secrets of God's Best Life for You

When Jesus came to earth more than two thousand years ago, He fed the hungry and healed the sick. He lived among us and died for us. His motive was love, and His primary goal was our redemption. But as God Himself in human form, He also revealed God's character—His ethos—so that we could take it on ourselves, with His help and through His power. As Scripture says: "Imitate God, therefore, in everything you do, because you are his dear children."[11]

That's what an ordinary man named Simon did. Simon's personality did not hint at future success. He was impetuous and prone to extremes: bold or even violent one moment, fearful the next. But when he crossed paths with Jesus, he began to change. Simon gained a new name—Peter—and a new life.

Peter achieved much. He delivered Jesus' message to huge crowds. He performed miraculous healings. He boldly stood up to the religious leaders of the day. Inspired by God, he wrote some of the most important words in the Bible. Peter discovered his destiny—God's best life for him. He was successful because he submitted to the Lord's plan for him and allowed God to transform his life. He changed from the inside out.

Each of us is called to greatness: to resemble, reflect, and reveal the character of God. We *resemble* Him when we take in the ideals, attitudes, and attributes of our Creator and make them our own. We *reflect* His image when we notice our changing ethos emerging in our behavior. We *reveal* God to the world when people around us see the image of God in our lives. When we acquire His character, we acquire the power to have a positive impact not just on our own lives but also on those of everyone around us.

This is our best destiny, our ultimate purpose. This is God's best life for us. In following it, we become the people we were created to be.

The apostle Peter wrote the words that provide the foundation for this book.[12] In the second of two letters to the early Christians in the decades after Jesus' resurrection, he encouraged them to grow in godly character. He said, "God has given us everything we need for living a godly life. We have received all of this by coming to know him, the one who called us to himself by means of his marvelous glory and excellence. And because of his glory and excellence, he has given us great and precious promises."[13]

What is Peter telling us? That by growing closer to God and knowing Him better, we find all we need for living a godly life—for discovering our God-given destiny. That if we seek Him, He promises to show it to us.

We will have it, Peter continues, when we develop the ethos of God in eight specific dimensions of our character:

> In view of all this, make every effort to respond to God's promises. Supplement your *faith* with a generous provision of *moral excellence*, and moral excellence with *knowledge*, and knowledge with *self-control*, and self-control with *patient endurance*, and patient endurance with *godliness*, and godliness with *brotherly affection*, and brotherly affection with *love* for everyone.
>
> The more you grow like this, the more productive and useful you will be in your knowledge of our Lord Jesus Christ.[14]

Peter, Jesus' friend and a leader of the disciples, is giving us the secrets of God's best life for us. We must respond to God by becoming more like Him. This is what we were created for—to conform our lives to the character and ethos of God so that we can step into a future that is greater than anything we've imagined.

We do this by allowing Him to strengthen these eight essential pillars of our ethos:

Faith (Belief)
Moral Excellence (Virtue)
Knowledge (Wisdom)
Self-Control
Patient Endurance (Perseverance)
Godliness (Sacredness)
Brotherly Affection (Kindness)
Love

To help us grab hold of these eight pillars, let's briefly look at them in contrast to the negative qualities they will replace in our character when we embrace God's ethos. Because it's true that we were created in the image of God to reflect His character, the following statements also are true:

- We were not created for doubt and fear. We were created for *faith*.
- We were not created for immorality, depravity, or decadence. We were created for *virtue*.
- We were not created for ignorance. We were created with the capacity for *knowledge* and *wisdom*.

- We were not created to be slaves to destructive habits, our circumstances, or our surroundings. We were created for *strength* and *self-control.*
- We were not created for impatience. We were created for *patient endurance*, *perseverance*, and *purpose.*
- We were not created for irreverence. We were created to hold in great respect all that God says is *sacred*; and yes, we were created for *worship.*
- We were not created for meanness and cruelty. We were created for *kindness.*
- We were not created for hatred. We were created for *love.*

I believe these eight qualities represent the best in human character, bestowed by God on humanity. Each is a dimension of His ethos that He asks us to pursue. It's important to remember that God would never ask us to be what He is not. Whatever God asks us to be, He already is—perfectly so. These dimensions reside in their fullness in the character of God, as we can see throughout Scripture.

In the chapters that follow, we will explore each of these eight qualities. Some may already be strengths in your life. Some may be weaknesses that God wants you to work on so you may know success from the inside out.

Maybe you're looking at these eight pillars and thinking, *I'm not perfect, but I think I already have godly character. Why doesn't my life feel fulfilled?*

That's what this book is about. We'll discover that each element of the character of God not only must be developed to its full potential, but also must work in harmony with the other elements. These characteristics are intended to be cumulative. As the Scripture passage says, we supplement each quality with the next—faith with virtue, virtue with wisdom, and so on. They complement each other. If we have wisdom without kindness, for example, we may be harsh in the way we share our knowledge with others—and that doesn't faithfully represent God's character. These qualities work together to create a powerful whole.

Maybe you're looking at the eight pillars of ethos and wondering where you stand on each. You're thinking, *I'm generally a kind and loving person, but I do sometimes struggle with self-control.* Or, *I know I have a good moral foundation, but I'm not sure that my faith is as strong as it should be.*

Does it matter? Absolutely! Acquiring the ethos of God can make the difference between an undistinguished life and stepping into your best destiny. This is the key that opens the door to God's best life for you—and not just for you, but for families, businesses, societies, and even nations.

Change won't happen overnight. Growth is a process, and it requires deliberate planning. We won't heal or change in any area of our lives until we assess, diagnose, prescribe, and implement corrective measures. Isn't that what you do when you skin your knee? You *assess* your injury—it hurts, so you decide it needs further attention. You *diagnose* the problem—your skin is scraped and bleeding. You *prescribe* a treatment—your wound needs cleaning and protection. You *implement* a solution—you wipe away the blood with a clean washrag and apply a bandage.

We'll go through the same series of steps to help you develop the character of God. This process is essential to success. It is where God's best life for you begins.

God's ultimate best is His character, His ethos. When His character is in you, you will live His best life for you. You'll begin to reap some of the benefits we talked about earlier: confidence in your choices, hope for the future, fulfillment in your work and everyday tasks, powerful influence on those around you, peace that surpasses understanding, joy despite your circumstances, and a strong sense of purpose that brings renewed excitement to your life. Like Peter, a one-time fisherman who became the leader of the disciples, you will discover the life you were meant to live.

Are you catching a vision of your potential? Are you seeing an opportunity to break out of numbing normalcy? I hope so! This book is only the beginning.

BECOMING YOUR BEST YOU

How involved is God in your life?

What is your definition of greatness?

In what ways do you think you are modeled after God?

Which of the eight pillars of God's character seem the most natural to you? Which might be the most difficult for you to attain, and why?

God, thank You for giving me everything I need to live Your best life for me. I want to find it; I want to experience the best You have for me. As I begin this journey, please help me to allow You to work in me. Amen.

3

THE POWER OF BELIEF

How to Harness the Power of Faith to Change Your Life

This is going to be a disaster, Ana thought, watching her coworkers make their way into the room. I hate public speaking. Why did I get picked to give this training session? She cleared her throat nervously and rechecked her laptop. PowerPoint was up and running, her notes were in front of her, and her glass of water was waiting within reach. Her stuff was ready, so why didn't she feel prepared? "Hi," she said weakly to the people settling into the front row. "Ready to learn about the new inventory system? I hope this isn't too boring." She looked away and cleared her throat again.

It was just about time to begin when Ana's friend Sophie pulled her aside. "All set?" she asked.

Ana bit her lip. "I guess so. It's just . . . I'm not very good at this."

"Ana," Sophie said, a little impatiently, "you're giving the training because you understand this system better than anyone on the team. You built this software. I know you will do just fine." She turned and walked toward her seat before adding, "Have some faith in yourself."

Have faith in yourself? It sounded so simplistic that Ana almost laughed. But it was true that she knew the ins and outs of this program. Maybe she could manage to explain it. *I think I can do this*, she thought as she squared her shoulders and turned toward the group.

• • •

Some things have to be believed to be seen.

RALPH HODGSON

Buried deep in human nature is a treasure, the first secret to God's best life for us. Everyone has it, but most of us fail to appreciate or develop it. What is this treasure? It is the power to *believe*, and it is one of the most important and far-reaching faculties of human beings.

The power to believe, as well as the ability to choose *what* we believe, shapes our lives, circumstances, character, behavior, and destiny—our ethos—more than any other single factor. It is only our ability to believe in what we can't see that allows us to relate to God at all.

Do *you* appreciate the incredible potential of belief?

Heather Stepp McCormick does. In 1991, Heather was a sophomore on the University of Georgia gymnastics team. While warming up on the vaulting horse for a meet in Salt Lake City, Heather fell. She put her arm out to prevent landing on her head, and the violent collision with the floor broke her elbow.

Back home in Georgia, a medical official explained the severity of her injury. Muscles, tendons, and ligaments were all torn. "It was a mess, typically career ending," he said. "Our first thoughts were not gymnastics but to get her a usable elbow."

Doctors inserted a screw to reattach the ulnar collateral ligament. They told Heather she had just a 5 percent chance of fully extending her arm again, let alone regaining the hyperextension and strength required for gymnastics. If she agreed to allow doctors to put her arm in a cast, it would diminish her pain. But it would also end the small chance she had of continuing her gymnastics career. If she chose to forgo the cast, on the other hand, she faced excruciating pain and a lengthy rehabilitation. Yet she would also maintain that slim chance of competing once again.

Logic dictated that Heather should give up her gymnastics

dreams and choose the cast. But Heather didn't believe in logic. She believed in herself.

"I came to Georgia to be on a national championship team," she said, "and I'm not leaving without being on one!"

Heather rejected the cast and worked every day in grueling physical therapy sessions with her boyfriend (now husband), Matt. Mobilization and range-of-motion exercises gave way to strength and flexibility drills. She even carried weights while walking to classes on campus.

Perhaps to everyone's surprise but Heather's, by the next season she had not only straightened her arm but also regained her place on the gymnastics team. In fact, she was better than before. Heather was the team MVP and a first-team All-American in three events. She placed second nationally in the all-around and was national champion in the vault, the event that led to her injury.

Heather's top goal eluded her, however. She and her teammates just missed the team title, coming in second to national champion Utah.

Yet Heather didn't stop believing. She had one more season to achieve what had seemed impossible not long before. Her conviction rubbed off on her teammates. In 1993 Georgia became the first team in the history of collegiate women's gymnastics to record an undefeated season, prevailing at nationals with the highest team score ever recorded to that date. Heather added a personal exclamation point by winning national titles in the vault and floor exercise.[1]

It happened first and foremost because Heather believed it would happen. Her determination shaped her training decisions, her attitude while competing, and the way she interacted with her teammates. Her belief paved the way.

Scientists and psychologists often have a hard time with belief. It's been that way since at least the 1600s, when French mathematician and philosopher René Descartes proposed that the mind and body were entirely separate. He theorized that the mind was made out of an unidentified but immaterial substance that could not influence physical bodies made out of matter. Descartes favored scientific analysis to probe the unseen. Whatever could not be measured—including the spiritual world and the source of belief's power—was devalued or dismissed. That attitude has prevailed among many educated thinkers ever since.

Minds Working Miracles

Today, many of us still dismiss mysteries and perspectives that we can't easily account for. Because the explanation for the influence of belief is not test-tube verifiable, it is not considered worthy of discussion. Too many wizards of science and philosophy view faith as a weakness rather than a strength. They see it as a response to the insecurities and anxieties generated within us by our instincts and our experiences. To the skeptics, faith in God, or in a positive outcome when evidence does not support an optimistic result, is little more than an inexpensive way for us to self-medicate when faced with the fears and insecurities of life.

Yet when pressed, even these skeptics will admit that strong beliefs can lead to dramatic results. In fact, the beliefs we adopt have such an enormous impact on our behavior and lives that, even if something is not true originally, it often still *becomes* reality. This is true on both basic and profound levels.

For example, you may go to the movies and be not the least bit thirsty. But if the movie is *Lawrence of Arabia* and it features nearly two hours of hot, dry desert scenery before intermission, you'll likely find yourself joining the rest of the audience at the refreshment counter. In fact, record numbers of beverages were sold during the original airing of that 1962 classic.[2] Why? The influence of the movie experience caused people to adopt a false belief—that they were desperately thirsty. The suggestion was so strong that the belief became true. When the lights in the theater went on, the audience really did feel parched.

You have probably observed this in your own life. You're taking a walk on a summer evening, and your spouse mentions that it's getting cool. Suddenly, you wish you'd brought a jacket. You wouldn't have noticed otherwise, but now that the thought is in your head, you believe it: *I'm cold.*

More significant is the placebo effect. This is the phenomenon where you apply a treatment that you perceive will help your problem, and it then *does* help even though the treatment has no proven therapeutic benefit. Studies have shown that placebos can successfully treat a host of diseases, including asthma and Parkinson's, as well as depression.

To the shock of participants in a 2002 Baylor School of Medicine study, the placebo effect can even apply to surgery. Dr. Bruce Moseley, the study's lead author, wanted to know which part of his surgeries for patients with debilitating knee pain was giving them relief. Patients in the study were divided into three groups. For the first group, Moseley shaved damaged cartilage from each patient's knee. For the second group, he flushed material considered damaging from the knee joint. The third group got "fake" surgery—Moseley made three standard incisions, talked as if he were performing the actual surgery, and forty minutes later sewed up the incisions. All three groups were prescribed the same postoperative care and exercise program.

Moseley was stunned to discover that patients in the fake surgery group recovered just as well as those in the other two groups. "My skill as a surgeon," he said, "had no benefit on these patients. The entire benefit of the surgery for osteoarthritis of the knee was the placebo effect."

One member of the placebo group, Tim Perez, had to walk with a cane before his "surgery." Afterward, he improved enough to play basketball with his grandchildren. "In this world, anything is possible when you put your mind to it," Perez said. "I know that your mind can work miracles."[3]

Whether we can measure it or not, belief matters. What does all this have to do with becoming our best self? Everything. If belief in ourselves or in a placebo is that effective, just imagine how powerful faith in the living Creator can be! Having faith that He exists—that He is present and available—is the first step to becoming more like Him. When you combine belief with God's plan for your future, you take the first step into God's best life for you.

Belief in What Is Right and True

As you might expect, belief is a central theme of the Bible. It is one of the qualities that God values most—and the first dimension of the ethos He requires of us.

By definition, faith is "the confidence that what we hope for will actually happen; it gives us assurance about things we cannot see."[4] When we possess a highly developed gift for belief, we—unlike the skeptic or scientist—remember that so much of life has to do with what we cannot see: the air we breathe, the money that we're told is in our bank accounts, the amazing future we've yet to experience. We're confident that it's there even if we can't observe it or touch it.

The process of arriving at a belief works something like this: We listen with our hearts and interpret with our minds what is being presented for consideration as truth. We then run what has been presented through many filters—our culture, rationality, sensibility, prior knowledge, personal judgment and preferences, experience, and learned wisdom. We consider assumptions and suppositions. Only then do we offer the idea under consideration to our will, which decides whether or not to embrace it as belief.

After what has been introduced to us as truth navigates that gauntlet successfully and passes through the filters that reside in our conscious minds, we can decide to accept it. When most of our doubts have been processed and conclusions drawn, a *belief* is born.

Often, however, we fool ourselves about our beliefs. Our mouths say we believe when our hearts feel less certain. Our outlook is more like that of the disciple Thomas.

You've heard of "Doubting Thomas"? He was the guy who—after learning from his fellow disciples that his Lord and Savior, Jesus, had risen from the dead and appeared before them—said, "I won't believe it unless I see the nail wounds in his hands, put my fingers into them, and place my hand into the wound in his side."[5]

Isn't that how you and I so often respond to great news? We're afraid of dealing with disappointment, so we reject it unless we're presented with the physical goods. Thomas had walked with Jesus, listened to Him teach, and seen the miracles. He should have been ready to believe in a resurrection. Yet fear got the best of him.

For the next eight days, he refused to accept what his comrades told him.

What a week that must have been. I imagine the rest of the disciples talking excitedly with each other, barely able to contain their joy or the smiles on their faces. After the apparent tragedy of Jesus' death on the cross, all their hopes had been affirmed. God was real! He had risen! They *knew* this changed everything and would transform their future.

Except for Thomas. I wonder if he avoided the other disciples during those eight days. When they practically skipped by his doorway, did he duck back inside? Did he try to occupy his mind with chores during the day? Did he have trouble sleeping at night? Did he pray fervently to the Lord for faith, or did he harden his heart? Thomas must have sensed that his skepticism was separating him from the others—and from the life of faith he was born for.

This, my friend, is where you and I often live—trapped between doubt and hope, ducking into doorways because we don't want to confront the possibilities. God's best life for us proves elusive because we don't want to get burned.

Some of us exist in this netherworld for a lifetime. Thomas had to endure it for only eight days. He had rejoined his friends in a locked room when Jesus reappeared once again. Turning to Thomas, Jesus said, "Put your finger here, and look at my hands. Put your hand into the wound in my side. Don't be faithless any longer. Believe!"

Perhaps trembling, Thomas put out his hand and touched what he thought could not be touched. Jesus wasn't just an apparition or spirit. He was real, flesh and blood. Thomas got it. He exclaimed, "My Lord and my God!"

Christ's response was a message not just to Thomas but to you and me as well: "You believe because you have seen me. Blessed are those who believe without seeing me."[6]

You caught that, right? "Blessed are those who believe without seeing." In other words, when you believe in what is right and true despite not having the physical evidence, you will be blessed.

Notice that truth is a critical ingredient in the recipe. No amount of positive thinking or faith that you are ten feet tall will help you when you're actually half that size. On the other hand, resisting a powerful truth out of fear that you might be wrong will forever limit you. Don't be afraid to embrace a daring reality if it holds up to the scrutiny of your filters. Faith in what is right and true will change your ethos. It will allow you to develop the first essential quality of God's best life for you: *belief.*

You Become What You Believe

If you think about it, you will see that nearly every good thing that happens to you and me depends on the power of belief. You exercise and eat well because you believe it will make you feel better and will help your body last longer. You work hard at the office because you believe your efforts will be noticed and rewarded. You support and serve your spouse because you believe it will strengthen your marriage and that your love and commitment will be reflected back to you.

Success is not possible without faith in potential change for the better. When you link that belief with the power of God, anything is possible.

This is what two blind men learned when they followed Jesus and begged Him for mercy and healing. They must have heard about this amazing man of God and the miracles He could perform. They might even have been present for one of Jesus' miracles. But could they see it with their own eyes? No. They had to trust their ears and their hearts. They had to believe.

The blind pair followed Jesus indoors. When they approached and explained what they wanted, He asked them the crucial question: "Do you believe that I am able to do this?" Jesus didn't query the men about their background, their families, or their political connections. He didn't ask what had caused their blindness or how long they'd been afflicted. Only one question mattered: "Do you believe?"

Their answer affirmed their sincerity: "Yes, Lord."

Jesus touched their eyes and said, "According to your faith let it be done to you."[7] Suddenly, they could see.

Another version of the Bible paraphrases the passage this way: "He touched their eyes and said, 'Become what you believe.'"[8] That is the power of faith. It can transform each of us into a new person, into exactly what we believe. Unfortunately, this power can also lead us down negative or destructive paths.

I know a man named Jerry who auditioned for the part of town mayor for his school play when he was in fifth grade. Jerry and several other students performed a scene for their teacher, the play's director. The scene didn't go well—Jerry and several of the other kids forgot their lines. The teacher, exasperated, listed all the things that went wrong with the scene. All that Jerry remembered, however, was his teacher's anguished cry: "The mayor was *terrible*!"

In that moment, Jerry formed false beliefs that stayed with him for decades: He could not act. He was useless on a stage. When the pressure was on, he would not remember what to say. For years after, whenever Jerry was at a party or in a crowd of people, he rarely spoke, because he was afraid of making a fool of himself.

It happens all the time. A child is told she's stupid . . . or ugly . . . or lazy. If she hears it often enough—or even once by someone whose opinion she respects—she begins to believe it and lives her life accordingly.

You may know exactly what I'm talking about. Chances are that you're carrying a few false beliefs around with you every day. Those beliefs are damaging because the longer we live with them, the more we internalize them as truth. Our belief can take a false statement and turn it into reality.

We fight this battle against false beliefs throughout our lives. Advertisers tell us that we won't be happy unless we lose weight via their diet program. An out-of-town friend tells us that we need to be more supportive even though we've called every day that week. We lose an important client and tell ourselves that we can't succeed in this line of work.

The way to overcome false beliefs is to replace them with faith in the truth. We are all on a search for truth. Life without it is like a ship without an anchor—rudderless, aimless, and adrift, a fundamentally dangerous condition of existence. We must have truth we can stand on, truth we can believe in with every fiber of our being.

This is why we must identify and embrace what we believe. I'm not talking about belief in which football team will win this weekend. I'm referring to the most important beliefs of all—what we think and feel in our hearts about God.

Three Core Truths

I don't know where you are in your spiritual journey. I don't know whether you call yourself a believer or whether you're still seeking to define your faith. What I firmly believe, however, is that to achieve God's best life for you and discover your best destiny, you must accept three core truths:

- You were made in God's image,
- God loves you, and
- God has a plan for you.

Let's take a closer look at each one.

God's Marvelous Workmanship

You already read in the previous chapter that God created you to reflect His ethos. This is why David could sing in a psalm: "You made all the delicate, inner parts of my body and knit me together in my mother's womb. Thank you for making me so wonderfully complex! Your workmanship is marvelous—how well I know it."[9]

What God creates is marvelous. You were made to resemble what is holy, pure, and perfect. Cracks in your character have developed over the years from the battering of the storms of life in this broken world. False beliefs have seeped into your system and warped your outlook. It is vital to remember that the imperfections you see now were never part of your original blueprints.

God's Love

Patrick Morley once wrote about a father and son—Phil Littleford and his twelve-year-old son, Mark—who flew by seaplane to a secluded Alaskan bay to fish with two other men. The next morning, when the group tried to take off, the plane managed only a low, circular pattern. They realized that one of the pontoons had punctured and was filled with water. It was dragging the plane down.

The seaplane crashed into the water and capsized. Everyone was alive, but they couldn't find any safety equipment. After a prayer, the three men and Mark jumped into the bay to swim to land. The water was icy cold and the riptide strong. Two of the men managed to reach the Alaskan shore, but when they looked back, they saw Phil and Mark on the horizon, arm in arm, as they were swept out to sea. Though Phil may have been a strong enough swimmer to have made it to shore on his own, he wasn't going to leave his son behind to drown. Phil chose to die with his son rather than live without him.[10]

This is how much God loves you. He wants to be with you so badly that He would die for you. That is precisely what He did on the cross. Everything selfish, unkind, self-righteous, and wicked stood between us and God. But Jesus took it all upon Himself. When we believe in Him and what He did for us, we can be forgiven. Never forget the depth of that love.

God's Plan

You've probably heard of "helicopter" parents. These are the moms and dads who are always hovering over their children, so overprotective and quick to point the way that their kids never get a chance to learn about and experience life for themselves.

God isn't like that. He gives us the freedom to make good or poor choices. But God is certainly not indifferent, either. He has detailed plans for you and me, tasks and roles meant specifically for us.

This is why you'll find Scripture passages such as these:

- "'For I know the plans I have for you,' says the LORD. 'They are plans for good and not for disaster, to give you a future and a hope.'"[11]
- "For we are God's masterpiece. He has created us anew in Christ Jesus, so we can do the good things he planned for us long ago."[12]
- "There has never been the slightest doubt in my mind that the God who started this great work in you would keep at it and bring it to a flourishing finish on the very day Christ Jesus appears."[13]

Don't think for a moment that God doesn't care about your future. Whether you are His cleanup hitter, starting pitcher, or utility player, He has a spot for you on His team and a plan for using you to the best of your ability.

At this point, you may be thinking, *Oh yes, Wintley, I agree with all of that. I'm a Christian. I go to church, pray, and read my Bible. I believe all those things about God.* But I'm not talking about a casual belief, the kind where your favorite sandwich is turkey one week and pastrami the next. I'm referring to an unshakable faith, one so deeply embedded in your heart that it can be described only as truth. Remember Thomas? Despite the time he'd shared with Jesus, despite all that he'd seen and heard, Thomas would not accept what his heart and mind were telling him about the resurrection of Jesus. He had enough evidence to believe, yet he was unwilling to fully commit to it.

How about you? When you examine these three truths about God, what do your heart and mind tell you? Is your belief more like a favorite "flavor of the month," or is it so certain that nothing can shake it from its foundation? If you're not sure, you need to find out, because your chance to discover God's best life for you depends on it.

Let's talk about how you can determine the depth of your belief—and what to do if you discover it's only skin-deep.

Developing a Fully Committed Faith

Remember our discussion about what you do when you skin your knee? It's a simple yet effective way to break down most of the challenges we face in life. We're going to apply the same process to a different kind of challenge—your ability to believe in God's influence on your life.

When a child runs down the sidewalk, trips, and scrapes her knee, what is the first thing she does? She stops to *assess* the situation. She unconsciously asks herself a few questions: *Should I keep running or do I need to take a closer look? Does my knee hurt? Is this going to interrupt my playtime?*

It's time for you to do the same thing for the three core truths about God. Let's stop so you can ask yourself some slightly different questions: *Do these truths matter? Are my beliefs about these truths bringing me joy or pain?*

The next step for the little girl on the sidewalk is to *diagnose* the problem. When she takes a closer look at her knee, she sees that the skin is broken and bleeding. When you take a closer look at your beliefs, what do you find? Do you genuinely believe that you are made in God's image, that God loves you so intensely that He would die for you, and that He has a plan for your future? If you can wholeheartedly say yes to all three, then you have a faith that will sustain you in the toughest times. If not, however, it's time to stop ignoring the situation and do something about it.

Next, the little girl examining her wound decides to *prescribe* a treatment—she knows she needs to stop the bleeding, clean her knee, and find a way to protect her injury. What will you prescribe for your wounded spiritual state? You need to stop the damage caused by doubt and false beliefs. You need to respond to God and ask Him to clean your soul. You need to protect your heart and faith.

Finally, the little girl with the bloody knee takes steps to *implement* a solution. She walks home, gently cleans out the wound, and covers her knee with a bandage. What can you do to implement a resolution to your spiritual dilemma? You can start by examining the evidence of the Bible, the lives of genuine believers around you, and what you sense in your heart. You can confess your lack of faith to God. Last but certainly not least, you can protect your heart by infusing it with truth. Read Scripture, memorize it, and meditate on it until it is an inseparable part of you. Then ask God to help you believe with all your strength.

This is what the father of a demon-possessed son once did. The father brought his boy to Jesus, hoping for relief after years of torment. "Have mercy on us and help us," the father said, "if you can."

"What do you mean, 'If I can'?" Jesus asked. "Anything is possible if a person believes."

I can almost hear the mixture of anguish and hope in the father's immediate reply: "I do believe, but help me overcome my unbelief!"[14]

Here was another man trapped in the shadow world between faith and unbelief, a man so much like you and me. Jesus released the son from the demon's influence, rewarding the father's desire for a fully committed faith.

God stands ready to do the same for you. When you overcome your unbelief and activate belief's power by trusting in Him, you will begin to know Him. And that's the critical first step as you discover what it means to resemble, reflect, and reveal the ethos of God.

The power of belief made all the difference for my friend Barry Black. You may know him as chaplain of the US Senate, the first person of color to hold this prestigious position. What you may not know are the long odds he faced on ever reaching his destiny.

Barry was born in Baltimore's inner city, the oldest boy in a family of eight children. He was raised primarily by his mother, as his father was a truck driver and an alcoholic, rarely seen by the family. Their neighborhood was characterized by crime, drugs, and poverty. Cockroaches infested their home. Debris littered the streets. Domestic violence often served as the evening entertainment.

Barry often came home bruised and bleeding from encounters with hoodlums in the streets. During one fight, someone hit him in the head with a baseball bat. He learned to walk with "ghetto swagger" to show potential attackers he would be difficult prey. He also began carrying most of his money in his socks so that when people robbed him, he could pretend to have only a few coins in his pocket.

Once, when he was in eighth grade, Barry returned from school to his home in the projects to find all of his family's furniture on the sidewalk. Their landlord had evicted them because they'd failed to pay the rent. They had nowhere to live.

Most of the kids growing up in the inner city faced a future of incarceration, addiction, or early death. From all outward appearances, Barry's prospects did not look any better.

But Barry had a weapon against the hopelessness around him. He possessed the power of belief. He expected the unexpected.

Barry's mother, Pearline Black, passed on to her children the belief that God had great plans for their lives. She and other members of their extended family backed this optimism with cheerful diligence and often encouraged each other with Bible verses like this one: "Now all glory to God, who is able, through his mighty power at work within us, to accomplish infinitely more than we might ask or think."[15]

Thanks in part to this faith foundation, Barry gave his life to God when he was just ten years old. It led to a joy and peace that helped him battle the challenges of the ghetto with confidence. His faith enabled him to continue to expect the unexpected.

Barry's love for God deepened. He decided to become a preacher. After graduating from seminary, he learned about a need for military chaplains. Despite the advice of church colleagues to stay where he was, Barry decided to join the US Navy.

Barry was not done with expecting the unexpected. He sensed God urging him to believe in the "impossible." During a morning devotion while serving as a chaplain in Pensacola, Florida, he uttered an unusual prayer: "Lord, no black man has ever been the chief of Navy chaplains. If you decide to do this, I'd like to be the first."[16]

Ten years later, that dream became reality. Today, in addition to serving as US Senate chaplain, Barry is a retired two-star Navy admiral who holds doctoral degrees in ministry and psychology and has been decorated with the Navy Distinguished Service Medal, the Legion of Merit Medal, meritorious service medals, and Navy and Marine Corps commendation medals. His rise from the 'hood to Capitol Hill hardly seemed likely all those years ago, yet by engaging the power of belief, Barry Black changed his course. He adopted an ethos that aligned with God's and discovered his best destiny.

What's even more exciting is that God is inviting you to do the same.

God's Belief

Remember, your ability to believe depends on faith in God and His power. By believing in Him, you are becoming like Him, because He is the ultimate believer. When God believes, He dreams that planets are born—and they are. When God believes, He dreams that stars appear in the sky—and they do. His belief in His own creative power causes flowers to spring forth from the earth, and seeing His glory, they blush in Technicolor. God's belief in Himself has brought about all that we see, hear, and touch, as well as all we cannot see, hear, or touch. The universe we live in was built from the timber of His creative imaginings.

God created human beings in His own image. He believes in the quality and potential of His original workmanship—and that includes you. When you become willing to see yourself through His eyes, when you allow Him to reveal His perfect plan for you, you honor Him as the master artist and become more like Him. He wants you to become all that He has created you to be. If God believes in you this much, how can you believe anything less?

Belief is the first step toward a better life and all the powerful potential of your ethos. It is the spiritual hand with which you touch eternity. It's one of the eight pillars of God's best life for you.

As any architect knows, however, you need more than one pillar to build an unshakable foundation. Please keep reading as we explore the next secret of true success.

BUILDING BELIEF

When you grow your godly character, you discover wonderful by-products that better position you to succeed in life. Below are just a few of the positive qualities that can be both prerequisites of the dimension of belief and the result of developing your ability to believe. How many of the following qualities do you already possess? Which do you need to cultivate further?

Childlikeness—Children share the traits of innocence, trust, and frankness. Did you carry a certain childlikeness into adulthood?

Confidence—A person who has the ability to believe and be believed is a confident person, someone who trusts in his or her inner resources as well as in circumstantial provision. Are you inherently confident?

Conviction—Once birthed, a belief is very difficult to alter or destroy. This unshakable assurance can be called conviction.

Creativity—Since we were created in God's image, it is reasonable to conclude that we also can be creative. How creative do you feel you are?

Energy—A strongly held belief impels a person in a specific direction, often with significant force. A person cannot be energetic without holding some clearly defined opinions.

Happiness—The dictionary defines happiness as "a state of well-being characterized by relative permanence, by dominantly agreeable emotion ranging in value from mere contentment to deep and intense joy in living, and by a natural desire for its continuation."

Hopefulness—A hopeful person anticipates the best, is cheerfully expectant about the future, and hopes for success and a positive outcome.

Inspiration—Two signs that you have the capacity to believe and be believed are the abilities to be inspired and to inspire others.

Optimism—An optimist always sees the bright side of a situation and its possibilities.

To find out more about each of these qualities and to further investigate the power of belief in your life, I invite you to go back to our website at www.YourBestDestinyAssessment.com and take the assessment, if you haven't already. It will give you a greater understanding of where you are strong in this dimension of your ethos and where you need to focus more attention. Your answers to the quiz are clues that will help you pursue your dreams and achieve your best destiny, so answer as honestly as you can. On page 221 of this book, you can see the questions from the assessment that will measure belief.

BECOMING YOUR BEST YOU

What is your definition of belief?

Why is it important, or not, to base your beliefs on a foundation of truth?

How do you respond to the three core truths? Are there any that you have a hard time believing? Why? How could you change that?

How do you think God exhibits belief?

Dear God, as I begin my journey of believing, I look to You to lead the way. Make me sensitive to Your voice of instruction and encouragement. Thank You for believing in Yourself and believing in me. Amen.

4

THE BEAUTY OF VIRTUE

How Doing the Right Thing Helps You Sleep Better at Night

Aaron rolled onto his back and stared at the ceiling. Every time he was almost asleep, he would jerk back awake as the thought ran through his mind again: *What if she finds out?*

It hadn't seemed like a big deal at first. He had spent hours trying to find sources for his sociology paper—the first big paper of his freshman year—but the college library hadn't had the books he needed. He couldn't figure out how to locate the right journal articles, and he had been too embarrassed to ask the library aide for help. Overwhelmed, he'd started to panic. He'd begun searching for sources online, and that's when he'd found it: another student paper on the same topic.

He hadn't copied all of it. Not much at all, really—just enough to fill in the holes in his research. And he'd gotten a B+ on his paper. It should have been over. But it had been hard to look his professor in the eye after that, and he hadn't been participating as much in class—not wanting to draw the professor's attention. Even now, two weeks later, it was like a constant refrain: *What if she finds out?*

• • •

The happiness of your life depends upon the quality of your thoughts: therefore, guard accordingly, and take care that you entertain no notions unsuitable to virtue and reasonable nature.

MARCUS AURELIUS

You could say that our society has a problem with virtue.

The Josephson Institute of Ethics recently assessed the morals of 43,000 high school students across America. Here's what they found:

- Eighty-nine percent of teens agreed that "being a good person is more important than being rich," yet more than 40 percent said they had lied to save money. Almost one-third of boys and one-fourth of girls had stolen from a store in the past year.
- Ninety-two percent agreed with the statement "I am satisfied with my own ethics and character," yet 80 percent had lied to a parent about something significant, almost 60 percent had cheated on a test, and 34 percent had copied from the Internet for a school assignment.
- Forty-seven percent said they had "been bullied, teased, or taunted in a way that seriously upset" them, yet 50 percent had bullied, teased, or taunted someone themselves.
- Seventy-nine percent agreed that "when it comes to doing right, I am better than most people I know," but almost 40 percent agreed with the statement, "A person has to lie or cheat sometimes in order to succeed."[1]

Rather disturbing, wouldn't you say? And yet, where do our young people learn these unscrupulous attitudes and behaviors? From their parents and other role models. In other words, from you and me. When it comes to virtue, it seems our modeling is lacking.

Virtue—purity of thought and action—is a vital dimension of character that keeps us from becoming slaves to what is wrong. Virtue helps protect us from impure thoughts and actions. It is an important check on the selfish desires that are in us all. Virtue (or integrity) is the guardian at the gate, the sentinel within the soul.

Virtue is also the second essential pillar of God's ethos. When you and I develop a fullness of virtue that resembles, reflects, and reveals His, our lives change for the better. Because of the moral choices we make and the trust we build, our personal and professional relationships grow stronger and deeper. When others trust our character, we are granted increasing responsibilities. Our sense of fulfillment expands along with our influence. When we follow God's standards for right and wrong, we don't have to live with a sense of unease, afraid of being found out and always aware that we are not living with full integrity. Instead, we are at peace. In short, when virtue becomes part of *our* ethos, we take an important step toward discovering God's best life for us.

We exhibit virtue through actions that demonstrate high moral standards. When we look around ourselves, however, we so often see examples not of virtue but of a society with seemingly no standards at all. Politicians are ensnared by scandalous affairs and cases of corruption. Pastors fall prey to the lure of pornography. Athletes ingest illegal steroids and other substances to enhance their performance, then lie about it. Marriages break up over moral indiscretions with friends, neighbors, and even other family members.

Lying. Cheating. Stealing. Adultery. This is certainly not what we would call reflecting God's character. The guilt and the consequences for our reputation and our relationships are far from worth it, yet these stories are all too common.

What is wrong with us? How did we get here? C. S. Lewis, in his 1943 book *The Abolition of Man*, might just as easily have been referring to us today when he wrote, "We make men without chests and expect of them virtue and enterprise. We laugh at honor and are shocked to find traitors in our midst."[2]

When Lewis says "chests," he's talking about the core of our being: the heart. Something important is missing inside of us. It is our ability to discern and act on what is right and wrong. It is a problem with our ethos, and it's blocking us from being who we were created to be.

An Essential Part of God's Ethos

We can trace this problem all the way back to the Garden of Eden. Adam and Eve's choice to disobey God led to a world infected with wrong motives, wrong thoughts, and wrong actions. Even so, we start out with a moral conscience. Young children are highly concerned with establishing what is good or evil and what is true or false. It is why they are so often drawn to fairy tales that teach clear lessons in ethics. Our kids have the gift of what author Vigen Guroian calls a "moral imagination." As he puts it:

> Every parent who has read a fairy tale to a young son or daughter is familiar with what I venture to say is a universal refrain of childhood. "But is he a good person or a bad one?" Or, "Is she a good fairy or an evil fairy?" What greater proof or assurance could we want that God and nature have endowed human beings with a moral constitution that needs to be nurtured and cultivated?[3]

This gift of moral imagination is not just a happy accident. It is, by design, part of God's plan to encourage us to be more like Him.

The Bible is full of references to God's holiness and righteousness. Everything He does is true and right. But if you have any doubt that virtue is an essential part of God's ethos, all you have to do is look at the life of His Son, Jesus Christ. In the Bible, we read no accounts of illicit affairs, of pocketing profits, of payoffs to keep whistle-blowers quiet. In fact, when the Jewish leaders were trying to convict Him of a crime, they were unable to find proof of any wrongdoing—so they had to find witnesses who would lie.[4] Jesus was so sure of His moral status that He challenged His opponents with the statement, "Which of you can truthfully accuse me of sin?"[5] Even His final earthly judge, the Roman prefect Pontius Pilate, said of Jesus before sentencing Him to death: "He is not guilty of any crime."[6] The writer of the book of Hebrews concurs, saying that Jesus was tempted as we were—but did not sin.[7]

It is also important to note that Jesus took on the most upright people of the day, the Jewish keepers of the law called Pharisees. He could have found easier targets. The Greeks and Romans practiced ritual prostitution. Corruption was rampant. Care for the poor was minimal. Yet Jesus—God on earth—chose to point out the flaws of those who considered themselves outstanding spiritual and moral examples: "What sorrow awaits you teachers of religious law and you Pharisees. Hypocrites! For you are like whitewashed tombs—beautiful on the outside but filled on the inside with dead people's bones and all sorts of impurity."[8] Jesus made it clear that our standard is to not merely *look* virtuous but *be* virtuous.

I once read about a man who looked virtuous. This man drove up to a fast-food outlet and bought two fried chicken dinners for himself and his date. The attendant was distracted, however, and unintentionally handed over the proceeds from the day's business—a bag of money (much of it cash) instead of a bag of fried chicken. After driving to their picnic site, the couple sat down and opened the bag, only to discover over eight hundred dollars.

Many people would have rejoiced in their good fortune and kept the money, but this man got into his car and drove all the way back to the restaurant. Mr. Clean became an instant hero when he returned the money to the frantic store manager. The manager was thrilled and wanted to call the local newspaper. "I'm gonna have them come take your picture. You're one of the most honest men I've ever met," the manager said. To this, Mr. Clean quickly responded, "Oh, no, no—don't do that!" Then he leaned over the counter and whispered, "You see, the woman I'm with is not my wife."

What looked like virtue on the outside turned out be something else on the inside.

Maybe we need to pattern ourselves after rock candy. If you see a stick of candy with the words "Brighton Rock" embedded on it, you might expect the letters to disappear after you suck away the first half inch. Not so. No matter how much you lick, you can still see the words. The letters run all the way through the candy.

We were designed to have integrity running all the way through us. Yet it all went wrong. Our virtue is more like a movie set of a palace exterior—beautiful on the outside but fake and empty on the inside.

Small Compromises Mean Large Consequences

Part of the problem of our skin-deep morality is our postmodern culture. We live in a world where truth is often viewed as relative—that what works for me may be different than what works for you. Biblical standards are often dismissed as irrelevant or ignored altogether. Many see the ideals of high moral character as quaint, old-fashioned, even prudish. You may feel that way yourself.

The entertainment media doesn't help. Movies and television celebrate people who do what it takes to get the job done, even if the rest of their lives show little evidence of virtue (think playboy Tony Stark in the *Iron Man* movies). They show us people who lie, cheat, and steal to get what they want.

Virtue has become the homely, forgotten sister, the unappreciated protector of modesty, morality, and nobility. But the truth is, virtue is actually one of the primary qualities that distinguishes us as human beings from the rest of the animal kingdom. Almost everything we do in the physical world, animals can do just as well, many of them much better than we can. We can't run as fast, walk as far, or move as quickly. We can't fly at all. I read of a female Alaskan shorebird that flew 7,145 miles from Alaska to New Zealand without taking a break for food or drink. It was the longest nonstop bird migration flight ever recorded, and she did it in nine days.

As impressive as that is, human beings can imagine and complete things far beyond that little bird's ability. Like the God in whose image you were created, you have the ability to think, to plan, to arrange and rearrange. You have the ability to appraise and evaluate, to weigh and analyze, to reason and think logically.

That reasoning ability allows us to understand when we've done wrong. We know better. We want to follow God. Our minds tell us the logic behind virtuous living. Unfortunately, however, we occasionally let our guard down and make small compromises. And before we know it, the cesspool we live in sucks us in.

Immorality is a little like arsenic. If you include a small dose of arsenic in your diet every day, you won't even notice it. But over time, the toxic accumulation of poison will kill you.

God has been watching our struggle with virtue for a long time. I don't know what compromises King David was making before the evening on his rooftop when he spied Bathsheba bathing in her birthday suit, but I can guarantee that his thoughts were less than pure. On that fateful night, David could have immediately turned away from the enticing view and no harm would have been done. Instead, he allowed himself a little peek. Then he took a longer look. The more he lingered, the more lust filled his heart.

David asked about Bathsheba and learned she was the wife of a soldier named Uriah. He sent for her. He slept with her. When David learned that she was pregnant with their child, he gave orders to make sure Uriah was killed in battle. Then he married Bathsheba and began raising their son. His actions did not go unnoticed, however. The prophet Nathan confronted David, saying that God was displeased with him and that his son would die. After the son of David and Bathsheba suffered for a week with illness, that's exactly what happened.[9]

We still struggle with virtue today. Joe was the executive pastor of a growing church in Sacramento, California. He had a wonderful wife and two beautiful children. But there was one thing Joe was unhappy about: He felt he deserved a higher salary. He effectively ran the church and put in long hours to make sure everyone was served properly. The church was doing well financially. Yet Joe's request for a raise was turned down.

At first, the only thing Joe did wrong was to allow his bitterness over the situation to grow. Then he began to fantasize about a solution to his problem. Finally, he began to put his scheme into action. Each week, he began to take a small portion of cash from the offering to supplement his "inadequate" salary. In his mind, he rationalized what he was doing. After all, it was only a little money, and he felt he deserved it.

The day arrived, however, when Joe's deceit was discovered. He was immediately dismissed from his position. He'd lost his ministry and the respect of his friends and colleagues.[10]

Festering bitterness eventually led Joe to a life of persistent theft. David started down a path that ended in adultery, murder, and heartache. Maybe you've had a similar problem. A little justification here, a little rationalizing there, and suddenly your life is spinning out of control. The small moral compromises we make can have huge, tragic consequences.

This is not living by God's ethos. If we want to know His best life for us, we must put an end to compromise.

Not Even a Hint

My family will tell you that I always read the labels on the food we eat. My favorite notation is "100 percent." That tells me something has been packaged in its purest, most unadulterated form.

I want only 100 percent pure orange juice and 100 percent pure grape juice. I try to stay away from additives and preservatives. That's how I like it—100 percent. No contamination allowed.

Would you buy orange juice if it had dead bugs in it? Would you drink grape juice if it had a slick of oil on top? Of course not. So why do so many of us feel free to contaminate our minds? Why do we allow the purity of our thoughts to be tarnished and polluted by the evil around us?

All over the world, when wells and drinking water are left

uncovered and exposed, they soon become polluted. The same thing happens to you and me. It is virtually impossible to live in this world uncovered and unexposed. Our hearts too easily become polluted.

Are you getting the picture here? Even a little garbage will spread to every corner of your life and pollute your system. You need 100 percent purity.

That's what God tells us too. In the Bible, we read:

> Among you there must not be *even a hint* of sexual immorality, or any kind of impurity, or of greed, because these are improper for God's holy people.[11]

Not even a hint. We're not talking about cutting back on immorality. We're not suggesting that going on an "impurity diet" will solve the problem. What is needed is total virtue—a wholehearted, uncompromising commitment to high moral character.

Impossible, you say? You're right—if we rely only on our own strength. It doesn't work to try to muscle our way through on determination alone. We need God's help, and even then it's not easy. I'm certainly still working on it. We must start by listening for God's voice and by recognizing that success requires absolute dedication.

Years ago, I was in Washington, DC, waiting for an elevator. When the doors opened, I saw that the car was full. "Go ahead," I said. "I'll catch the next one."

"Where are you going?" one of the people in front asked.

"To the west steps of the Capitol."

"That's where we're going too. Squeeze on in."

I didn't see any room for me. I still felt inclined to let them go on without me. But something told me I'd better squeeze in. Little did I know that God was at work.

Once I jammed my way into the small space and the doors closed, I heard a voice from the back of the car: "Wintley Phipps, you don't realize how much your music has been a blessing to my life. My name is Sam Brownback."

I knew that Sam Brownback was a US senator from Kansas, but I didn't expect him to know me. The voice continued.

"Hey, Wintley, what are you doing tomorrow?" he said. "In the Capitol rotunda, we're giving a Congressional Gold Medal to Mother Teresa. I'd like for you to come and close the program by singing 'Amazing Grace.'"

That is how I had the opportunity to meet and sing for Mother Teresa, whose lifelong commitment to serving the poor, the sick, and the unloved has inspired me and millions more. She founded the Missionaries of Charity, which began as a small order in Calcutta with just thirteen members. By the time of her death, it had grown to include more than four thousand sisters operating orphanages, AIDS hospices, and charity centers around the world.

In a 1999 Gallup poll, Americans chose Mother Teresa as the most admired person of the twentieth century. This was a woman who lived by the ethos of God, a woman who demonstrated love and compassion to the world, a woman who discovered God's purpose for her. Mother Teresa lived God's best life for her. She also understood that an unwavering commitment to high character—including virtue—was vital if she was to live out her best destiny. She and the other members of the Missionaries of Charity took vows of chastity, poverty, and obedience. Those vows kept them close to the people they served and to the God who guided their steps.

If you're married, you've taken a vow as well—to love, serve, and be faithful to your spouse. Even if you're not married, you've made certain promises to the people whom you're close to and whom you work for. Your commitment to those promises and to living a virtuous life means everything. It is essential to your character.

Five Courses of Action

Despite what your friends or the media tell you, old-fashioned virtue is always in style. Even in a world that thumbs its nose at anything virtuous or pure, you will not—you cannot—reach your best destiny without it. Why? Because when virtue is a priority for us, we become free. Free from guilt about wrong choices, free from a need to hide what we have done, free from fear of our sin being found out. We start living in the confidence of knowing we are doing what is right. When we fail, we can admit our wrongs to God and get back on track. When we fix our eyes on God's view of virtue, we begin looking beyond short-term pleasure to long-term good, and we find joy in living the way God intended. This is God's best life for us!

Once you have allowed God to thread virtue throughout your character, you will better know right from wrong. Even if you have squandered years of your life in unvirtuous living, you can make a new start. And if you have lived a basically good life but suspect you're missing something, quite possibly it is a resolute commitment to true integrity at a heart level, not just an external level.

What can you do to remedy a lack of virtue and develop godly moral character? I recommend five courses of action:

1. Choose a Life of Purity

A young man named Eric walked into a pastor's office and said he was mad at God. The pastor asked why.

"Because," Eric said, "last week I committed adultery."

After a long pause, the pastor said, "I can see why God would be mad at you. But why are *you* mad at *God*?"

Eric related that for months he'd felt a strong attraction to a woman at his office. He'd asked God to keep him from immorality.

"Did you ask your wife to pray for you?" the pastor said. "Did you stay away from the woman?"

"Well . . . no. We went out for lunch almost every day."

The pastor began slowly pushing a large book across his desk. As he pushed, he prayed, "Oh Lord, please keep this book from falling!"

The book reached the edge of the desk. The pastor kept pushing. The book fell to the floor with a loud slam.

"I'm mad at God," the pastor said. "I asked Him to keep my book from falling . . . but He let me down!"[12]

You and I may pray to God for help, but if our words are empty and don't match our true intent, we can't expect God to honor them. He promises to provide an escape from temptation—"When you are tempted, he will show you a way out so that you can endure"[13]—but we've got to play our part. When we see the way out, we've got to act on it.

To live a life of virtue, you must make up your mind that this is what you want. It is a conscious choice you make now and every time temptation arrives at your doorstep. God will give you what you choose to have.

2. Believe You Can Live a Virtuous Life

Virtue is an essential dimension of the character of God, but it will falter without the first dimension of His ethos: belief. You must not only choose a life of virtue but also believe that with God's help you can succeed in your choice. God Himself says, "The righteous shall live by his faith."[14]

Have you read Victor Hugo's classic novel, *Les Misérables*? Early in the story, an old bishop takes in a just-released prisoner named Jean Valjean. To Valjean's surprise, the bishop serves him a splendid dinner with his finest silverware, one of the old man's few possessions of value. Then Valjean is shown to a clean bedroom.

Despite the man's kindness, Valjean makes an immoral choice: He gets up in the middle of the night, stuffs the silverware into his backpack, and slips away. He is caught by the police, however, and is marched back to the bishop's house. Valjean knows he is doomed to spend the rest of his life in prison.

Then the bishop surprises Valjean again. "Oh! Here you are!" he says to Valjean in front of the stunned policemen. "I can't believe you forgot the candlesticks! They are made of pure silver as well. . . . Please take them along with the forks and spoons I gave you."

Thanks to the bishop's words, Valjean remains a free man. After the police leave, the bishop tells him, "Jean Valjean, my brother, you no longer belong to evil, but to good."

Valjean again faces a choice. Will he believe that he is destined for a life of crime or that he can choose a life of virtue? The bishop's faith and grace encourage him to believe in a better destiny. Valjean becomes the mayor of a small town, builds a factory, and gives jobs to the poor. He also takes pity on a dying mother and raises her daughter.[15]

Because he chose to believe in a life of virtue, Jean Valjean reflected the ethos of God. So can you.

3. Set Boundaries to Stay Pure

In the proper context, fire is a wonderful feature in our lives. It can warm our living rooms, help us cook our meals, and allow us to dispose of unwanted yard debris. Fire is safe in a fireplace. But outside of that fireplace, it can be harmful. When fire gets out of control, it can destroy lives. That's why we need boundaries to keep it where it belongs.

The same can be said about sex. Within the right context, it is one of God's greatest gifts to humanity, a pleasurable way to express and receive love. But when sex gets out of control, it can inflict terrible damage.

If you want to keep sex in its proper context, you need to take an honest look at yourself and set boundaries that will keep your life pure. I know of a man who stopped going into video stores because the movie covers created too much of a temptation for his eyes. Some families cancel their television or Internet service or put the family computer in a public room to limit opportunities to stray. Some married couples refuse ever to be alone with another member of the opposite sex.

The need for boundaries applies to other areas as well. If you are tempted to gossip and speak negatively about others, you might think about the people in your life who encourage you to do this and limit your time with them. If you struggle with fudging numbers on your taxes, you might ask your spouse or a CPA to prepare them.

We're all different. Boundaries will vary from person to person. Just don't fool yourself into thinking you're stronger than you are. Acknowledging our potential for wrongdoing and our need for God's help is one of the best things we can do to protect ourselves. Take steps now to establish boundaries and live a life of purity.

4. Find an Accountability Partner

Anything we struggle with—whether it's being dishonest in our financial dealings, cutting corners at work, or not completing what we said we would do—will be more difficult to overcome if we are isolated. We need to be able to talk with others about our frustrations. We'll find it easier to live with integrity if we surround ourselves with people who have similar goals and values.

We shouldn't expect to live a life of virtue without help. Make it a priority to ask someone you trust (preferably of the same gender) to be an accountability partner. Plan to meet regularly with this person, and encourage him or her to ask the tough questions: Any struggles with integrity this week? How are you doing with your thought life? What is tempting you lately?

When we go it alone, we put ourselves at risk. But when we have an accountability partner, we're twice as strong.

5. Treasure Virtuous Thoughts

As we've already seen, the health and well-being of humans depend on a system of water purification that is efficient and reliable. In the same way, your spiritual health depends on virtue to function as a purification system, a filter against corrupting influences. Once it is poured into the foundation of your character, virtue will cleanse, disinfect, and sanitize whatever seeks entry into your mind and heart.

Whether you realize it or not, every day contamination seeps into the well of your mind and heart. Every day, you face a constant barrage of polluting images, and whatever gets into your well will manifest itself in your words and behavior. Compromised and corrupted by this pollution, the reflection of God in your mind and heart grows tarnished. Your delight for beauty, your perception of loveliness, and your appreciation of simple gifts and pleasures diminish in proportion to the pollution you have allowed to enter.

What can you do about it? With God's help, you must purify your mind and heart. You must screen your thoughts for pollutants and discard those that don't belong so that what remains is as pure as clean water from a deep well. You can do this by confessing your impure thoughts and acts to God and asking for His forgiveness. The Bible says that when we seek His forgiveness, God is "faithful and just to forgive us our sins and to cleanse us from all wickedness."[16]

Someone once said, "You are not what you think you are, but what you *think*, you *are*." In large part, the person you are today is the result of the thoughts you have nurtured throughout your life. If you want to change your conduct and behavior to reflect goodness and decency, you must feed your mind with virtuous thoughts.

The Bible puts this simple yet profound wisdom like this:

> Fix your thoughts on what is true, and honorable, and right, and pure, and lovely, and admirable. Think about things that are excellent and worthy of praise.[17]

Try it and you will see how effective this strategy can be. When you are tempted to lie, think about the truths God has revealed to you. When you feel inclined to gossip, remember the people who have behaved honorably toward you. When your gaze starts to linger and turn into lust, ponder what is pure and innocent in your life—a newborn baby or the love of your family.

In fact, don't wait until you're in a tough spot. *Always* fix your thoughts on what is true, honorable, right, pure, lovely, admirable, excellent, and worthy of praise. Treasure these thoughts. Store them in your heart. When you do, you will find there's little room left for immoral imaginings. Your "well" will sparkle with clear water and your very presence will bring refreshment to others.

What Virtue Looks Like

We've talked a great deal about the problems caused by a lack of morality and the steps you can take toward a more virtuous life. You may be asking, "So what does a life of integrity look like? How does adding this pillar of God's ethos help me pursue my best destiny?"

Centuries ago in Egypt, for a man named Joseph, it worked something like this:

As a slave, Joseph was put in charge of the household of Potiphar, the captain of Pharaoh's guard. While Potiphar was away, however, his wife took a fancy to Joseph. "Come and sleep with me," she said. Joseph refused, saying, "How could I do such a wicked thing? It would be a great sin against God."

Day after day, Potiphar's wife kept up the pressure on Joseph. Finally she grabbed his cloak and demanded, "Come on, sleep with me!"

Joseph didn't give in. Seeing no other options, he ran from the house.

In the short term, Joseph's virtuous choice didn't pay off. The scorned wife accused him of rape and he was thrown in prison. But God blessed Joseph for his moral character. He eventually became Pharaoh's most trusted representative and was put in charge of not just the palace but all of Egypt.[18] Everyone respected and obeyed Joseph. His character attracted the attention of men and the blessing of God. He discovered God's best life for him when he reflected God's ethos.

In modern times, choosing virtue may look something like this:

Bill Hackett was the president of Steelcase, an office furniture company. Steelcase began selling a new line of products, including panels designed to be used either for office cubicles or as floor-to-ceiling walls. Company officials learned, however, that the material was not up to fire standards when it was used as floor-to-ceiling walls.

It didn't seem like a big deal. "We had not had one damaged installation," Hackett said. "Our customers even called us and said, 'Oh, don't worry about it. What you're worried about, no one will ever have a problem.'" Since fire codes vary, the product's fire-retardant level probably would have been enough to meet standards in some areas.

But Bill Hackett didn't let it go. It didn't feel right to forget about it. He didn't want there to be any question about meeting fire standards. So Steelcase recalled all the panels and replaced them with ones that met stricter fire codes, at a cost of $40 million. Hackett and the rest of the company's executives lost their bonuses that year.

Then, on September 11, 2001, a terrorist-controlled jet liner crashed into the Pentagon, also blasting into the improved, more fire-retardant Steelcase product. "It was determined," Hackett later said, "with all the jet fuel and fire, if the new Steelcase material was not there, the fire would have spread in a far more disastrous outcome."[19]

Today, Bill Hackett goes to bed each night knowing he did the right thing about a product that wasn't quite up to standard—and knowing that he probably saved lives because of it.

You can't put a price tag on peace of mind. It is just another benefit of stepping into God's best life for you.

A Holy Satisfaction

Real joy begins when you cultivate virtue. Remaining virtuous for a lifetime requires a lifelong covenant, and you can make that covenant today. With a full embrace rather than a tentative hug, welcome everything that virtue has to offer. The passing pleasure of immorality is nothing compared to the lasting fulfillment found in living by the ethos and character of God.

Pastor and author John Piper speaks of this fulfillment when he writes:

> The fire of lust's pleasures must be fought with the fire of God's pleasures. If we try to fight the fire of lust with prohibitions and threats alone—even the terrible warnings of Jesus—we will fail. We must fight it with a massive promise of superior happiness. We must swallow up the little flicker of lust's pleasure in the conflagration of holy satisfaction.[20]

There is a holy satisfaction that comes when we choose a life of virtue. Wouldn't you like to know that satisfaction? Then put virtue in control. Today is the day to decide that you want virtue to go everywhere you go and purify your every thought and act.

When you are filled all the way through with virtue, you begin to fulfill your amazing destiny as a child of God.

THE VALUE OF VIRTUE

Virtue, or integrity, purifies the air you breathe. It is your 24/7 sentinel committed to lifelong vigilance. Virtue is your faithful soldier-watchman, guarding your soul from the temptations that stream in through your eyes, ears, and other senses. It is the radar that warns of invading and corrupting influences. Virtue stands guard over your imagination and keeps watch over your heart.

It's time to look at the prerequisites and by-products of virtue, those signs that virtue is constantly on patrol. As you consider each one, think about the strengths and weaknesses of your moral character. Ask God to help you develop this dimension of your ethos so that you can more closely resemble, reflect, and reveal His.

Honesty—An honest person is known for being truthful and living with integrity. He or she is fair and straightforward.

Modesty—Modesty walks hand in hand with humility. A modest person is aware of his or her personal limits and does not seek attention.

Morality—The backbone of the virtuous is their commitment to morality. Far from being boring and bland, a moral life is filled with beauty and purity, characterized by goodness and even godliness.

Nobility—Nobility stands for gracious dignity, a sense of excellence and value that is carried with confidence, and an ability to command resources for the sake of others.

Obedience—A life lived in obedience to the call of virtue is a life of beauty and purity, not of slavish servitude.

Prudence—A prudent person displays a timeless quality of caution and good sense, showing appropriate restraint in his or her decisions.

Purity—Inner purity is reflected in outer actions. It describes someone who is spotless in spirit, soul, and body.

Selflessness—A selfless person is generous and sacrificial, devoid of egotism. Do you usually think first of yourself or of others?

Sincerity—People close letters with the word "sincerely," but do they really mean it? A sincere person is not only honest, he or she is also free from hypocrisy and shades of truth.

To further explore each of these qualities and to better understand the value of virtue, go to our website at www.YourBestDestinyAssessment.com. You'll find resources to guide you as you cultivate a godly character and become the person you were born to be. If you haven't yet taken the assessment, we encourage you to do so. On page 225 of this book, you can see the questions from the assessment that measure virtue.

BECOMING YOUR BEST YOU

How does God help (or not help) you live a virtuous life?

What is your personal definition of virtue, based on your life experiences?

Why is it important to understand and appreciate virtue?

How do you think God displays virtue?

Dear God, I need virtue to be alive and well in my heart and life, and I know I need Your help to do that. Show me what to do and how to keep doing it. Thank You for Your perfect love, which makes everything possible. Amen.

5

THE JOY OF WISDOM

How to Make Better Decisions

Michael shook his head as he looked at the credit card statement. On top of the regular stuff—gas; groceries; clothes for Jasmine and Caleb, who seemed to be growing constantly these days; and too many trips to the hardware store to fix the most recent home-repair disaster—he'd spent way too much on takeout again this month. But by the time he got the kids off to school, worked a full day, ran a few errands, and picked up the kids from after-school care, he was too exhausted to think about cooking. He still had homework and baths to deal with before he could finally call it a night.

He loved his kids more than he could express, but being a single dad was tough. Sometimes he wondered if he would be better off moving back to his hometown. His sister had told him she would watch the kids after school, and his mom would like nothing more than to cook for them a few nights a week. Being around their grandparents would be great for Jasmine and Caleb. But could he find a decent job there? And even if he could, was it worth uprooting everyone? New house, new schools, new friends—that was a lot of change for a six-year-old and an eight-year-old to handle. *I need wisdom*, he thought. *What is the best thing for my family?*

• • •

Trust in the LORD with all your heart;
do not depend on your own understanding.

PROVERBS 3:5

A MOTHER NAMED PATSY calmly explained to her thirteen-year-old daughter, Kathleen, why she couldn't buy and wear a short leather skirt like all the other girls in her class.

Kathleen did not want to hear it. Three times she pleaded her case: "If I don't have this skirt, I'll be left out. And all my friends won't like me." Three times Patsy said no. Kathleen ran upstairs and slammed her bedroom door.

Patsy's husband was working that evening, so it was entirely up to her to handle the conflict. She'd won the battle but felt like she was losing the war. She wondered if she was doing the right thing.

Then an inner voice gave Patsy the affirmation she needed. It said, simply, *Hold fast!*

Kathleen appeared at the top of the stairs and demanded the skirt. Patsy again said no to her request.

Just when Patsy thought the matter was finally settled, Kathleen stomped down the stairs. "Well," the frustrated teen announced, "I'm just going to tell you one more time—"

With her hands on her hips, Patsy interrupted her daughter. "Do not answer," Patsy said. "Do not say anything. Turn around and go to bed. And do not make a single sound!"

Kathleen turned around. Patsy, meanwhile, spent the next several minutes staring at nothing, waiting for her blood pressure to go back down. Then she heard the creak of an upstairs door.

Now in pajamas, her eyes red from crying, Kathleen once again descended from the top of the stairs. Her steps were softer this time. When she reached the bottom, she held out her arms to Patsy.

"Oh, Mom, I'm sorry," she said. "I was so scared!"

"Scared of what?" Patsy asked.

"I was scared that you were going to let me win!"

Patsy was confused, but only for a moment. She had passed

an important parenting test. Despite what she said she wanted, Kathleen knew deep down it would be better for her if she didn't buy the skirt—and if her mother held to her convictions. Patsy had made the right choice when she listened to the wisdom of that inner voice.[1]

Wisdom. It is essential for moms dealing with strong-willed daughters. In fact, it is a critical dimension of character for all of us if we want to enjoy success in life. Once we develop belief and virtue that begin to resemble, reflect, and reveal God's ethos, we must add wisdom in order to know His best life for us.

But what exactly is wisdom? Where does it come from, and how do we get it?

The philosopher Francis Hutcheson once wrote, "Wisdom denotes the pursuing of the best ends by the best means." Wisdom has also been described as "knowing what you don't know as well as what you know." Some of us seem to add wisdom as we age and go through the trials of life—yet many people suffer greatly without ever becoming wiser. So how can we be sure we are developing wisdom?

When I crack open a dictionary and look up *wisdom,* here is what I read: "Accumulated philosophic or scientific learning: knowledge. Ability to discern inner qualities and relationships: insight. Good sense: judgment."[2] Those three featured words grab my attention: *knowledge, insight,* and *judgment.* It will help us on our journey to take a closer look at each.

The Value of Knowledge

Just as your body needs exercise to remain fit, so does your mind. It's easy to relax and allow others to do your thinking for you, but people with strong character also possess strong minds. They have a thirst for the knowledge needed to succeed in life.

My good friend Ray is one of these people. Ray grew up without a father in New Britain, Connecticut, and spent six years in an orphanage. When he was sixteen, he lied about his age so he could drop out of high school and enlist in the army. When he got out three years later, he was an uneducated man with few prospects. He took on two jobs, one at a factory and one at a gas station.

Ray may not have had much schooling, but he knew how to work hard and how to learn. He saved enough money to buy a gas station of his own at the age of twenty. Then he set out to improve his mind. Every day, after the early morning commuter rush, Ray cleaned up his gas station. Then he pulled out a series of newspapers—the local paper, the *Wall Street Journal*, and the *New York Times*. He wasn't a good reader, but he slowly made his way through stories about business and the world.

Often, Ray came across a word he didn't know. The next time a customer pulled in, Ray would fill the car with gas and wash the windshield. Then he'd tell the customer, "Wait one second!" He'd run into his office, grab the newspaper, and hurry out again. After thrusting the newspaper at the customer, he'd point to what he'd been reading. "What's that word?"

The customer would tell him. Then Ray would ask, "What does it mean?" The customer would explain that, too.

After a while, Ray found he didn't have to show his newspaper to customers so often. His knowledge was growing. He combined that knowledge with a strong work ethic and solid business instincts. Ray bought more gas stations and gradually turned them into a thriving regional empire. Today he is not only a multimillionaire but also a man of faith.

Knowledge is the vital first step toward acquiring wisdom.

Solomon, the great Israelite king and son of David and Bathsheba, is known as one of the wisest men who ever lived. He is credited with passing on these proverbs, as well as hundreds of others:

- Every prudent man acts with knowledge.[3]
- Whoever loves instruction loves knowledge.[4]
- He who has knowledge spares his words, and a man of understanding is of a calm spirit.[5]

Solomon understood the connection between knowledge and wisdom. We cannot make wise choices or guide others through their trials without a thorough knowledge of people, the world, and the facts relevant to whatever situation we face. We must acquire a comprehensive body of information and experience before we can begin to approach a place of wisdom.

We usually respect people with extensive knowledge: college professors, scientists, doctors, theologians, psychologists, financial analysts. We value the years of study and training they've invested in their chosen fields. We admire the perseverance they've demonstrated in acquiring their expertise.

Yet as valuable as knowledge is, it alone is not enough to bring about wisdom that reflects the ethos of God.

We know that Osama bin Laden was an educated man. He studied both economics and business administration at King Abdulaziz University in Saudi Arabia. Some reports indicate he also studied engineering and public administration. Yet bin Laden used his knowledge to form the terrorist organization al-Qaeda and plan the murders of thousands of innocent people.

Bernie Madoff was an educated man. He earned a bachelor's degree in political science from Hofstra University and also went to law school. His knowledge helped him become a stockbroker, an investment advisor, chairman of the NASDAQ Stock Market, and an icon on Wall Street who was trusted to manage investments for more than four thousand clients. Unfortunately, Madoff's knowledge also enabled him to operate the biggest Ponzi scheme in history, about $65 billion worth. He cheated thousands of people out of lifetimes of savings.

You can probably think of examples closer to home—bosses, teachers, friends, or family members who have used knowledge for misguided or selfish purposes. Clearly, all of our education and experience do us no good if they do not lead us in the direction of genuine wisdom.

Where Our Knowledge Ends

The best part of learning is that it teaches us where our knowledge ends and our ignorance begins. Here are the facts of the matter:

- The first step to knowledge is to realize that you don't know it all.
- What counts in knowledge acquisition is what you learn *after* you reach the point where you acknowledge that you don't know it all.
- Knowledge is like a snapshot: It can be enlarged, but if the values that should accompany it get out of focus, everything becomes a confusing blur.
- Knowledge without zeal is impotent; zeal without knowledge is fanaticism.

- Knowledge alone is useless on the battlefield of life.
- Knowledge is power only when it is turned on.
- Much of our knowledge is gained by learning humility and trust.
- Knowledge involves knowing a fact. Wisdom involves knowing what to do with that fact. Therefore, knowledge is like dynamite—dangerous unless handled wisely.

Remember the second word we identified in our definition of wisdom? *Insight.* If we want to be wise, we must apply insight to our knowledge. Our learning and experience can be put to good use only if we understand what we might do with it—and what God wants us to do with it. Insight involves discerning how we should apply our knowledge to the situations we face.

George Washington Carver, the scientist who developed hundreds of useful products from the peanut, said that when he was young, he asked God to share with him the mystery of the universe. But God answered, "That knowledge is reserved for Me alone."

So George said, "God, tell me the mystery of the peanut."

To that, God said, "Well, George, that's more nearly your size." And He told him the mysteries of the peanut.[6]

We should be thankful that God didn't grant George's first request! Human beings aren't equipped with the wisdom to handle the mysteries of the universe. But we can, with God's help, begin to understand what to do about the challenges we meet daily.

Sometimes the choices we confront aren't as simple as picking between right and wrong. Sometimes discerning God's will doesn't come easily to us.

A young woman named Allison worked full-time, as did her husband, Jared, in a fulfilling office environment. Both earned a similar, modest annual income. Allison enjoyed her coworkers and her duties as a communications assistant for her company. When their first child was born, Allison and Jared had to make a decision—should one of them quit work to stay home with their new son?

This wife and husband gathered all the facts they could. They talked to friends who had made one choice or the other. They read books on child rearing and the influence of stay-at-home moms versus daycare on children. They made budget projections for their family if their income was cut in half—a difficult dose of reality. They also read their Bible and prayed.

The knowledge gained from this effort was beneficial. It allowed them to use insight to identify three practical options: Allison could continue working full-time; Allison could quit her job to become a full-time mom; or Allison could approach her boss with the idea of reducing her hours so she would still bring in some income but also spend significant time at home with their son. This last option involved some risk, as Allison didn't know how her boss would respond to such a request. Her boss might decide that Allison was no longer committed to her job and look for a replacement.

All the research and discussion was beneficial to Allison and Jared in another way: It gave them new insights into their life priorities. They came to a clearer understanding of how much family and faith meant to each of them.

Allison and Jared now had knowledge and insight. They understood the advantages and disadvantages of the choices before them, and they had discerned how they might apply this knowledge to their situation. But to truly achieve wisdom, they needed to make a decision—one that lined up with the character of God.

Decisions That Lead to Wise Action

Another definition of wisdom goes like this: "Not simply knowing what to do, but doing it." In other words, making a wise *judgment.*

A judgment is the final decision formed after you've used discernment to compare various options. It is what a judge or jury does at a trial and what you and I do when we must make a difficult choice. It is a resolution that leads to wise action.

In the case of Allison and Jared, their final judgment was for Allison to approach her boss about reducing her hours. For this couple, it was worth the risk of Allison losing her job entirely because of their commitment to having at least one parent spending as much time as possible with their son. Because of their particular values and circumstances, it was the choice that their ethos demanded.

As it turned out, Allison's boss did approve the new plan. Allison continued working but also spent more time at home. Though Allison and Jared had to tighten their financial belts, they felt confident they had done the right thing for their family—the *wise* thing.

Knowledge leads to insight, which leads to judgment or decision. That's the road to wisdom and to our God-given destiny.

When I look at school systems in America today, I see us falling short in this process. I don't say this in any way as a put-down of our educators who work so hard. Yet the traditional, though unspoken, emphasis of modern public education continues to be on ranking students—through grades—rather than on corrective instruction and inspiring the light that comes with knowledge, understanding, and a love of mastery. This has become increasingly true as teacher responsibilities and class sizes have grown.

When we impart to each student not just knowledge but a love of learning and mastery of specific objectives, and we do so in a values-based program, we allow our young people to step closer to the vital character dimension of wisdom. This is our aim at the US Dream Academy. I founded the academy in 1998 after I performed in a number of prisons and was moved by the sight of tearful young children visiting their incarcerated parents. I didn't want those children to follow in their parents' footsteps. I desired a different kind of dream for them. Today we offer programs in eight cities, serving nearly a thousand students who are at risk of academic failure and a life in prison.

Skill building is the first pillar of a Dream Academy education, but we don't stop with helping our students acquire knowledge. The second pillar of our program is character building, with an emphasis on peace, love, truth, right action, and nonviolence. The third pillar for our students is dream building. We help them imagine and have hope for a future they might not have thought possible before. Community mentors play an important role in this pillar, as they help students understand the process that can turn dreams into reality.

Derrell Frazier was one of our Dream Academy students. A troubled teen, Derrell lost his brother at a young age and was one of ten children raised by his grandmother. He believed he was destined for failure. After he joined the Dream Academy, however, he met President George W. Bush and worked with mentors who helped show him what he might do with the knowledge he could gain at school.

Derrell eventually enrolled at Morgan State University, where he is pursuing a degree in philosophy. He also plans to attend law school.

We place our young people on the path to wisdom when we give them knowledge. We move them forward when we help them understand what to do with that knowledge—insight—and then teach values that enable them to take their future into their own hands by making wise judgments.

The finest gift we can offer, however, is to show them how to resemble, reflect, and reveal the wisdom of God.

Unlimited Wisdom

As we saw earlier, King Solomon was famous for his wisdom. You probably know the story of his judgment regarding a baby: Two women living in the same house came to him with one infant. Both had recently given birth. The first woman claimed that the second woman had accidentally smothered her child during the night, and then had stolen the first woman's baby while she slept. The second woman insisted that the roles were reversed and that *she* was the rightful mother.

Solomon listened to them argue for a time, then said, "Bring me a sword." When the weapon arrived, the king announced, "Cut the living child in two, and give half to one woman and half to the other!"

Before a servant could raise the sword, one of the women cried, "Oh, no, my lord! Give her the child—please do not kill him!"

At nearly the same time, the other woman said, "All right, he will be neither yours nor mine; divide him between us!"

Then the king said, "Do not kill the child, but give him to the woman who wants him to live, for she is his mother!" The story of the wisdom Solomon displayed to determine the baby's true mother spread and inspired awe throughout the nation.[7]

The king did not come by his wisdom through knowledge or experience alone. He received it from God after specifically requesting it. Early during his reign, Solomon was visited by God.

> That night God appeared to Solomon and said, "What do you want? Ask, and I will give it to you!"
>
> Solomon replied to God, "You showed great and faithful love to David, my father, and now you have made me king in his place. O LORD God, please continue to keep your promise to David my father, for you have made me king over a people as numerous as the dust of the earth! Give me the wisdom and knowledge to lead them properly, for who could possibly govern this great people of yours?"
>
> God said to Solomon, "Because your greatest desire is to help your people, and you did not ask for wealth, riches, fame, or even the death of your enemies or a long life, but rather you asked for wisdom and knowledge to properly govern my people—I will certainly give you the wisdom and knowledge you requested. But I will also give you wealth, riches, and fame such as no other king has had before you or will ever have in the future!"[8]

Do you understand what happened? God was so pleased with Solomon's request that He lavished incredible blessings on the new king. Because Solomon's desire was to serve his people rather than serve himself, God granted his request and much, much more.

This is an example for you and me. Want to know how to get out of debt? Need help with reaching your drug-addicted child? Want guidance on where to turn for dealing with your depression? You need wise counsel—not the kind of advice that the grocery-store butcher is always giving out but the kind that comes from an almighty, all-knowing Creator.

From my days as a young boy that I spent dreaming of piloting powerful jet planes, I have been fascinated by flying machines. In my study at home sits a model of one of the early Delta jets. When I get up close to it and focus my eyes, I can see every tiny detail; the cockpit, the wings, or the engines fill my vision. When I step back, I can take in a view of the entire jet at once. But I can't do both. My vision is limited this way.

God operates on another dimension entirely. His view is both detailed and wide, both present and future. His knowledge, insight, and judgment cannot be questioned. As the Bible tells us, "The wisdom of this world is foolishness to God."[9] No matter how hard we look, we'll never find greater wisdom than His. It is His wise guidance that will propel us toward His best life for us.

When we seek God's wisdom, we begin to get a glimpse of His perspective on our lives and who we are in light of Him. Our priorities might shift. Our goals might change. We will find ourselves going deeper, using our time more effectively, and making better choices. We'll be reflecting God's character through our decisions.

What have we just learned in this chapter? That knowledge is the accumulation of facts, insight is an understanding of what we might do with those facts, and wisdom is the judicious use of both. Without knowledge and understanding, you cannot have wisdom, and without wisdom your knowledge and understanding will not take you where you need to go. So commit yourself to lifelong learning and ask God to teach you to wisely use the knowledge you gain. This will play a critical role in helping you fulfill your supreme destiny.

Some knowledge and understanding are gained by firsthand life experience and some are gained by purposeful study. The goal is never merely to accumulate facts but rather to go further by adding both insight and judgment. Knowledge is the raw material with which God crafts wisdom in each of us.

To discover a wisdom that will help you become the best *you* that you can be, consider these action steps:

- *Realize* that you do not have all the knowledge you need. Yes, really. The moment that you decide you know as much as you need to, your learning adventure will end.
- *Learn* humility and trust. This will allow you to look past yourself and put your confidence in God. Only then will you add insight to your knowledge.
- *Ask* God specifically for His wisdom. Wait for Him to speak to you through spiritual inspiration as well as doors of opportunity that open or close. Make sure the answer is His and not just what you want to hear—see your life through His eyes.
- *Act* on the answer you receive. A wise judgment remains just a theory unless you have the courage to put it into motion.

When you apply this kind of wisdom to your problems, you will soon find your life changing. Ideas will form that never occurred to you before. People will surprise you with welcome solutions. Perhaps best of all, as you move closer to an ethos that matches the character of God, you will know the kind of joy that Solomon describes:

> Joyful is the person who finds wisdom, the one who gains understanding. For wisdom is more profitable than silver, and her wages are better than gold. Wisdom is more precious than rubies; nothing you desire can compare with her. She offers you long life in her right hand, and riches and honor in her left. She will guide you down delightful paths; all her ways are satisfying. Wisdom is a tree of life to those who embrace her; happy are those who hold her tightly.[10]

You should understand by now that human knowledge by itself is an unreliable guide. Knowledge may be power, but it will be a power for good only when it is united with true understanding and wisdom. Knowledge must be enlivened by God or it will never serve a noble purpose.

All knowledge is treasured up in God's infinite mind. We need to acquire as much of it as we can—but only by looking steadily to Him and by acknowledging and applying His eternal wisdom.

WINNING WITH WISDOM

Wisdom is an incredible gift. It gives us the power to see things as they really are. It provides us with a deep understanding of truth—about ourselves, about other human beings, and about God. It allows us to distinguish between right and wrong, between good and evil, and enables us to act on that knowledge.

In addition, wisdom provides many other benefits. Examine the prerequisites for and benefits of wisdom below to discover which of these dimensions of character are already part of your life and which may need to be developed further.

Earnestness—When you are earnest, you are serious, industrious, and sincere, showing a firmness of intent. Do people notice this quality in you?

Efficiency—An efficient person can tackle the tasks of the day or week in an organized, competent, and effective manner, wisely marshaling all necessary resources.

Fearlessness—A fearless person operates out of an inner sense of valor. This results in risk-taking at its finest, as the fearless person trusts in God for the outcome.

Initiative—To show initiative means to take charge of a situation with enterprising resourcefulness. When was the last time you behaved this way?

Persistence—We admire people who persist. They have the resolve to solve problems and complete tasks regardless of obstacles.

Purpose—A wise person knows his purpose in life and how best to achieve it. Do you?

Resiliency—Resiliency implies strength under stress, flexibility, and durability. Wisdom teaches us that the resilient are more likely to be successful.

Responsibility—Think of the people you most respect. Are they accountable for their actions in a dependable, trustworthy manner? If so, they are responsible.

Thoroughness—The wise are also thorough, giving attention to details and concerned with achieving excellence in all things.

As with the character dimensions of belief and virtue, you can learn more about wisdom and how to make it part of your ethos by visiting our website at www.YourBestDestinyAssessment.com. On page 229 of this book, you can view the questions from the assessment that measure wisdom.

BECOMING YOUR BEST YOU

Do you feel you have a mature level of knowledge for your age? Why or why not?

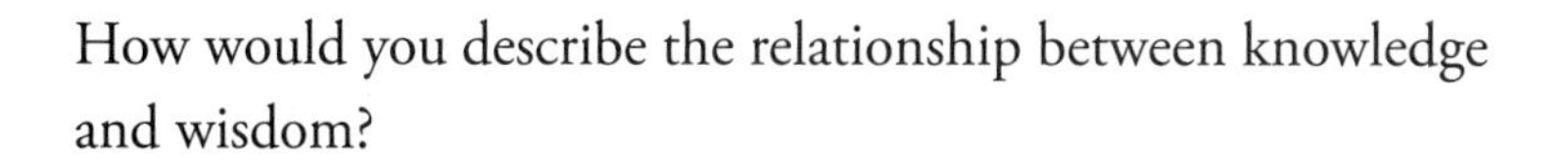

How would you describe the relationship between knowledge and wisdom?

Why is the acquisition of knowledge so important? Is all knowledge equally valuable? Why or why not?

Why is it important to grow in wisdom throughout life? How will you accomplish this?

Think about a decision you are facing right now. How could you implement knowledge, insight, and judgment to come to a wise conclusion?

Dear God, as I assess my level of knowledge and understanding, I can see that I have a journey ahead of me. Help me to hear Your voice of instruction. Show me where to concentrate my efforts. Thank You for opening my understanding. Amen.

6

THE STRENGTH OF SELF-CONTROL

How Willpower Keeps You on Track

Ben groaned as he looked at the clock. Another hour had gone by, and what did he have to show for it? He'd jotted down a few notes—but he also knew the score of every major league baseball game that had been played today, the weather for five different cities in his state, the Facebook statuses of all his acquaintances, and the world's major news headlines.

It wasn't that he did anything inappropriate online. It's just that he wasted so much time. And it was moving him further and further from his goal.

Ben had wanted to go back to school for years. He wouldn't complain about his job, really. Being the maintenance guy at a school might not be that exciting, but it gave him medical insurance and paid the bills if he was careful. That was nothing to take for granted in this economy. But what he really wanted to do was be a teacher. He had a heart for those kids he saw on the sidelines, the ones who shuffled through the halls looking as if they'd rather be anywhere but there. Ben remembered that feeling from his own days in school, and he knew he could make a difference.

This Saturday morning he'd gotten up early, grabbed his coffee, and headed to the library to start researching programs. But the choices felt overwhelming, and so here he was, sabotaging himself through sheer lack of willpower. How could he get back on track?

...

A person without self-control is like a city with broken-down walls.

PROVERBS 25:28

What would you call a man who can balance atop a pillar just twenty-two inches wide, more than eighty feet above the ground, without a safety harness—for thirty-five hours? Or a man who can lie entombed in a coffin with six inches of headroom, consuming nothing but water—for a week? Or a man who can hold his breath while submerged in a glass sphere filled with water, in front of a national television audience—for seventeen minutes?

The man who can do all these things is named David Blaine. This modern-day Houdini makes his living as a magician by performing physical feats that most of us would consider impossible. Mr. Blaine calls himself a professional endurance artist. I might call him crazy—but I would also describe him as a master of self-control. His ability to endure torturous circumstances without moving, eating, or even breathing—when he could put an end to his difficulties at any time—makes him a rare breed.

For most of us, self-control is an elusive concept. We live in a time when individual freedoms, affluence (or the desire to appear affluent), technology, and a society with an "anything goes" attitude have all combined to create a world that continuously challenges our ability to master our desires. All too often, we hardly put up a fight.

Consider, for example, the way we eat . . . and eat . . . and eat. We are surrounded by fast-food restaurants that promise convenience and by relentless advertising that pushes us to overfill our bellies. The result is that two-thirds of American adults are overweight, and nearly half of those qualify as obese. Bariatric surgery, which limits caloric intake by walling off parts of the stomach or removing part of the intestine, was nearly unheard of a generation ago. Today an entire industry is dedicated to the practice. More than two hundred thousand of these surgeries are performed in the United States each year.[1]

Our problem with self-control certainly isn't limited to food. Many of us have made it a habit to spend more than we earn. We're still trying to recover from the 2008 economic crisis, when people who borrowed against the inflated value of their homes suddenly found themselves in massive debt when home values crashed. Even more frightening are our problems with road rage and child abuse, not to mention our addictions to just about anything you can think of.

Rather than try to increase our self-control, we often seem to exult in our lack of it. Today's "reality" TV shows celebrate our excesses. Via a hidden camera, for example, *Cheaters* films people suspected of committing adultery. The *Real Housewives* series often highlights women who are notable only for losing their tempers, spending too much money, and gossiping about others. This has become the latest sport—watching people on television who cannot seem to control what they do.

Maybe you know someone who has a problem with self-discipline. He eats too much; she talks too much. Or maybe it's someone who has no control over emotions and switches from nice to nasty in ten seconds flat. He or she flips from engaged to enraged, from calm to cantankerous, from serene to incensed, from delighted to demonic, from laid-back to livid—in less time than it took you to read this sentence.

Or perhaps you have a friend who is sober on Friday but drunk on Saturday, Mr. Virtuous on Sunday morning but Promiscuous Joe the night before. People drive while intoxicated—no self-control. Leaders are exposed in financial-misconduct scandals—no self-control. Too often, as we pursue pleasure and try to avoid pain, we are caught in a web of indulgence and the vicious snare of addiction, all because we don't possess enough self-control.

Is there a person close to you who cannot control cravings, urges, crushes, or desires? Is that person *you*?

The issue of how well we display self-control is more than significant. Author Daniel Akst would say that our lives depend on it.

> Dangerous habits like smoking, eating the wrong things, drinking too much, and having risky sex account for more than a million fatalities annually in this country, or close to half of all US deaths. Most of these behaviors are undertaken by people who know that what they're doing is risky and in many cases—as with cigarettes—would prefer to act differently, despite a conflicting desire for one more smoke or cupcake or line of coke. To put those million early deaths in perspective: no armed conflict, present or past, accounts for as much carnage as our losing war with ourselves—not even World War II, in which there were all of 400,000 US deaths. With our helmets and lawsuits and regulations, modern-day Americans appear to be obsessed with safety. But as a people, we're embarked on a campaign of slow-motion suicide.[2]

Your struggles with self-control may not be as extreme as what we've just talked about. I can just about guarantee, however, that your tendency to put off what needs doing, or to say what's best left silent, or to look when you ought to look away has brought you trouble. How about it? Don't all of us, at times, experience weakness in our willpower?

Yet the truly successful—the people whose success is built from the inside out—not only learn how to master their emotions and behavior but also acquire a kind of self-control that resembles, reflects, and reveals God's. The Bible is clear that He has strong emotions, such as love for His people and anger toward evil. Yet God never allows His emotions to control His actions. Think how frightening it would be to serve a God like that! Instead, He does what is right and just no matter how He might feel. This is what you and I want.

So what is the secret?

The Birth of Self-Control

Most parents attempt to teach self-control to their children almost from the day they are born. When a bleary-eyed mother grits her teeth in the middle of the night at the sound of her toddler's cry and waits an extra minute or two before going to him, she's trying to train him in the art of self-discipline. The same is true of the dad who refuses to give in when his two-year-old screams for candy in the grocery store checkout line. (It's no coincidence that all those tempting sweets are located at a preschooler's eye level—the people in charge of product placement at grocery stores know exactly what they're doing.)

This reminds me of a story about a father who was shopping with a totally uncooperative three-year-old. As his dad wheeled him down the aisles, the toddler sat in a grocery cart and asked over and over for a candy bar. Another man overheard part of the conversation between father and son. "Now, Billy," the father said, "this won't take long."

As the man passed this pair in the next aisle, the little boy's pleas increased in both decibels and octaves. "Candy bar! Candy bar!" the toddler screamed. Yet the father kept saying, "Billy, just calm down. We'll be done in a minute."

The eavesdropping shopper couldn't help watching these two.

By the time they neared the dairy section, the kid was howling uncontrollably. The father was still keeping his cool. In a low voice, he said, "Billy, settle down. We are almost out of here."

When they reached the checkout counter, the father continued to display a calm demeanor. The boy, meanwhile, was trying to kick his way out of his seat. People stared as the father calmly repeated, "Billy, we will be in the car in just a minute and then everything will be okay." The man who'd observed all this was impressed beyond words.

After paying for his own groceries, the man hurried outside to catch up with this amazing example of self-control. The man watched the father tuck his son into his car seat and say, "Billy, see, we're done. It's going to be okay now."

The observer tapped the patient father on the shoulder and said, "Sir, I couldn't help but watch how you handled little Billy. You were amazing."

The father looked at him, puzzled. Then his expression changed as he understood. "Oh, no, sir," he explained. "*I'm* Billy!"

We all need help with self-control, including hungry toddlers and exasperated fathers. We'll try just about anything if it gives us the self-discipline we seek, even if it means talking to ourselves.

Some of us have been using the same techniques to master our impulses for nearly our entire lives. You may have heard about an experiment conducted more than fifty years ago known as the marshmallow test. A group of four-year-olds was put in a room. In front of each child were a bell and a plate with a marshmallow on it. A researcher explained that he would leave the room. If a child wanted to eat the marshmallow, he or she could ring the bell and would be allowed to munch down the treat. If a child waited for the researcher to return, however, he or she would be allowed to eat two marshmallows.

Some of the kids rang the bell and ate the marshmallow immediately. They didn't want to wait. Many, however, were able to hold out, some for as long as what must have seemed an endless fifteen minutes. How did they do it? Some distracted themselves by singing. Others turned their backs or imagined the marshmallows as something less tasty, such as clouds or cotton balls. Those who endured to the end received their doubly sweet reward.

What is interesting about this study is what researchers discovered twenty-five years later when they followed up with the same group of kids. The children who were unable to delay gratification had higher rates of behavioral problems both at home and at school. They didn't perform as well academically and had more struggles in their relationships.

The former four-year-olds who were able to wait to get that second marshmallow, however, turned out much differently. They recorded greater academic achievement, higher self-esteem, lower rates of substance abuse, and more satisfaction with relationships. These kids, now adults, were happier and more successful.[3]

We already know that self-control is an important—in fact, life-changing—dimension of character. But if our talent for self-control is already so evident at age four, is it even possible to develop this area of our character? Are we for the most part born with this ability, or is it something we acquire starting in our first years?

The answer may be a combination of both. Multiple studies, for example, have shown that children growing up in two-parent homes are generally more successful in life. According to authors Roy Baumeister and John Tierney,

> Even after researchers control for socioeconomic factors and other variables, it turns out that children from two-parent homes get better grades in school. They're healthier and better-adjusted emotionally. They have more satisfying social lives and engage in less antisocial behavior. They're more likely to attend an elite university and less likely to go to prison.[4]

Based on the long-term marshmallow test results, we know that this kind of success correlates with increased self-control.

The connection between two-parent families and more successful children could signal a genetic factor—a parent who leaves his or her family may have genes that favor impulsive behavior. But it also could be that children raised in two-parent homes generally have more eyes watching them, and so receive more training in developing the crucial quality of self-control.

Personally, I believe that regardless of our DNA or background, we all have the ability to master self-control. I have seen so many people do just that despite overwhelming obstacles. Yes, it's true that we all have a breaking point. It might be redheads or it might be raspberry pie, but each of us has a vulnerable spot where self-control falls apart—if we rely only on self.

Fortunately, we have another resource.

Unconditional Surrender

From the beginning of recorded time, God has exercised control over His creation. When He said, "Let there be light," there was light.[5] When He said, "Let the land sprout with vegetation," plants and trees formed.[6] And when God breathed life into the first man and woman, He gave them instructions: "Be fruitful and multiply. Fill the earth and govern it. Reign over the fish in the sea, the birds in the sky, and all the animals that scurry along the ground."[7]

Was there a problem with God's work? Not at all. He looked at what He had made and "saw that it was very good!"[8] Humans lived in harmony with each other and with God. They knew and lived out their best destiny, an existence that included perfect submission to their Creator.

The trouble started with a deceitful serpent, who suggested that humans ignore God's loving commands and make their own decisions. You know how that turned out. We've been fighting a battle for control ever since.

Something in us still listens to the serpent today. We like the idea of charting our own course, of forging our destiny. Simply put, we want control.

Yet our ability to control what we think and do is a bit of an illusion, is it not? No one can discipline himself all the time. Even David Blaine had to step off his eighty-five-foot-tall pillar eventually.

Who really has sovereign control over our world? Who is actually the only one qualified to rule over not just our lives but the entire universe? That's right, the one who created us in the first place.

We don't question a mother who decides what her toddler will eat or wear. We don't shout about injustice when the same mother gets behind the wheel of her minivan instead of the toddler. Mom is in control, as she should be. Her authority, wisdom, and experience far outstrip the toddler's. When her little tyke throws a temper tantrum in an attempt to get his way, we shake our heads and smile. *Someday he'll learn,* we think. *Someday he'll see that his mom really knows best.*

If only we were that mature in our attitude toward God. We must appear like toddlers in His eyes, throwing temper tantrums when we don't get what we want. We so often don't see or acknowledge that our Creator knows best.

What are you a slave to? Food? Lust? Power? Money? The past? Drugs? Alcohol? Bitterness? Jealousy? Anger? What are the triggers that cause you to lose self-control? What are you trying to say no to right now, or later today at dinner, or tonight when that phone call comes?

How does *self* control *self*? It can't do a very good job without God's help. Self-control means putting my "self"—my body, soul, and spirit—under His ongoing authority. It results in becoming an individual governed by God.

Yes, self-control means control of self. But who's got control of you? Your best self will choose to hand over the reins to God, who makes all things possible. This is the great irony—that we begin to master self-control only when we give control to God. This is where the dimensions of character we've already talked about come into play. We won't be willing to give control to God until we *believe* in His plan for our lives, until we're committed to doing what's right (*virtue*), and until we have the *wisdom* to trust that His way is best.

In *The Message*, a paraphrase of the Bible, Jesus tells His disciples, "Anyone who intends to come with me has to let me lead. You're not in the driver's seat; I am. Don't run from suffering; embrace it. Follow me and I'll show you how."[9]

God will show you and me the way too. Yet giving Him control is easier said than done. It takes courage. It takes commitment. It takes trust. You might even say it takes unconditional surrender.

A Japanese soldier named Hiroo Onoda knows something about our reluctance to surrender. On September 2, 1945, Japanese representatives aboard the USS *Missouri* signed documents that declared their surrender to Allied forces, officially ending World War II. A handful of Japanese soldiers, however, never got the message.

One of these men was Second Lieutenant Onoda. The year before, he'd been sent to Lubang Island in the Philippines with orders to harass the enemy and prevent attacks on the island. When US and Philippine forces landed on Lubang in 1945, Onoda and three comrades took refuge in the mountains.

Onoda was a proud man. He didn't believe Japan could lose the war. When he found leaflets stating that the conflict was over and it was time to surrender, he was sure it was a hoax.

Years passed. Onoda and his men stole food, burned crops, and killed at least thirty nationals. One soldier finally walked away and surrendered to authorities. Two others were killed in encounters with search parties and the local police.

> Incredibly, nearly three decades later, in 1974, a lone Japanese dropout discovered Onoda hiding out in the Lubang mountains. A few months later, the former student returned to Lubang with Major Yoshimi Taniguchi, Onoda's former commanding officer. There they again found Onoda. Only after Taniguchi read an official order declaring "individuals under the command of the Special Squadron to cease military activities and operations immediately" did Onoda realize he'd been fighting an unnecessary war for almost thirty years.

Onoda later wrote, "Suddenly everything went black. . . . I felt like a fool for having been so tense and cautious on the way here. Worse than that, what had I been doing for all those years?"[10]

None of us likes to surrender. We refuse to surrender to God out of pride, rebelliousness, and fear. What we find when we fully trust in Him, however, is peace, joy, and self-control. It is when we give control to God that He gives us the power to accomplish the "impossible"—including a newfound ability to manage our actions and emotions. Unconditional surrender leads us closer to the ethos of God.

A Habit of Submission

We've determined that your best self comes alive only after you surrender your desires to God, who knows you better than you know yourself and who wants your character to reflect His. So how exactly will you do that?

As in any matter when we seek to grow closer to God, it begins with prayer and becoming familiar with His teaching. What is especially crucial, however, is to make it a continuous process. The habit of submitting to God—of acknowledging that He is in charge and giving control over to Him—must become so instinctual that you hardly need to think about it. I'm not talking about day by day but rather moment by moment, during the good times and the bad. You train yourself to think about what God wants instead of what you want, how He wants you to respond to a situation instead of what would feel satisfying to you. And as you read the Bible, you pay attention to what it reveals of God's ethos and how that might affect your own choices. When you develop this kind of character, God will bless you with self-control when you need it most.

A former professional football star named Tim Brown recently made this discovery. Tim and his daughter pulled into the parking lot of a fast-food restaurant to get a burger. A young woman in another car, apparently feeling that Tim had cut her off, made an obscene gesture. Tim decided to ignore it.

When Tim got inside the restaurant, however, he noticed that the man who'd been sitting next to the woman in the car was now right behind him in line. In a polite voice, Tim said, "Hey brother, I apologize for going in front of you there, but you really should keep your girlfriend from flipping folks off. You just never know when it's going to be the wrong person. People get killed over that kind of thing."

To Tim's surprise, the boyfriend flew into a rage. "What you gonna do?" he shouted. "What you gonna do, bro?"

Tim turned around and began to walk away. He had no desire to get into a confrontation with a person who was out of control.

"Oh, you *better* walk away," the man said loudly.

Tim whipped back around. Suddenly, the competitive fire that had fueled a long and successful NFL career was blazing. Tim pictured himself teaching this guy a lesson—and maybe breaking his nose.

Yet Tim paused for an extra split-second. He knew he needed a second opinion on what he was about to do. Instead of pulling back his fist, he gave control of the situation to God—and quickly sensed that God wanted him to turn away once again. Tim found the strength to take a deep breath and sit down at a table with his daughter. His blood pressure dropped. The conflict was over.[11]

It's not always easy, but when we consistently turn to God's guidance for each and every circumstance, we find self-control we never knew we had. Handing control of our lives over to God will not only keep us from behavior that will derail our best plans, but it will also give us extra ammunition to reach new heights of success. We will discover new levels of concentration, of focus. Nothing will distract us from the future God has in store. Godly self-control is a power that propels us into our best destiny.

A woman I'll call Debbie grew up in a home with an alcoholic, controlling father. After the misery of that experience, Debbie promised herself that she would never again let anyone have power over her life.

When Debbie brought that attitude into her own marriage, however, it led to trouble. In an attempt to demonstrate that she—not her husband—was in charge of her life, Debbie turned to relationships with other men. Then she began abusing alcohol just as her father had. The harder Debbie tried to control her life on her own, the more out of control she became.

Twenty years into their marriage, Debbie's husband discovered the truth about her affairs. To her surprise, he offered mercy and tender yet firm leadership, including a plan that would allow Debbie to get her life back in balance.

The choice was Debbie's—continue to fight for control, or surrender to a better option? She chose the latter.

"I repented," she says. "I knew I had to submit completely to God and to my husband—in that order!"[12]

Debbie had always been afraid of what would happen if she gave up control of her life. Now, however, she began to encounter blessings she'd never imagined.

> A *huge* weight was lifted off my shoulders. I didn't want to be in control any more. My journey has not always been easy, but it has been wonderful and life-changing. I had to "let go" of a lot of people in my life—but I have God and my family. I have a beautiful peace of mind and serenity. And I hold my head high every day, because I know I have been forgiven. I will never be the same person again—ever.[13]

Debbie's motto changed from "I am in charge of my own life" to "Your kingdom come; Your will be done." By letting go of the reins, Debbie developed the self-control to end the affairs and her alcohol abuse. Her marriage improved dramatically. At long last, she had stepped into the life she was intended for—a life that would resemble, reflect, and reveal the ethos and character of God.

Do you want that kind of life too? Then give control to Him—and watch what happens.

Success with Self-Control

True self-control is impossible without God's help. He is the only one with the power and authority to control your entire life in all of its physical, moral, and spiritual aspects. Not only does He have the power and authority to do it, but He's also loving enough to want to. All you have to do is allow Him the chance. We need Him working with us every second of every day in order to attain the best destiny He has planned for us.

God wants your character to reflect His, and He's more than willing to help you. Once you surrender your right to yourself to Him, He activates your self-control. As you keep on dying to self-centeredness and returning to Him, every aspect of your character will flourish and grow.

FINDING SELF-CONTROL

God is the one true source of self-control. Once we surrender ourselves to Him, the power to control our character is activated. As long as we reject our selfish ways moment by moment and return to Him, we will grow in both strength and depth of character.

The truly great men and women in this world possess godly self-control. It is a dimension of character that keeps all the other dimensions in check and balance.

How do you measure up in terms of self-control? Is it bringing balance to your life and character? As you read through the following prerequisites for and by-products of self-control, look for anything that might be keeping you from becoming your best self and achieving God's best destiny for your life.

Decisiveness—A self-controlled individual has no trouble being decisive. Firm and confident, such a person can resolve questions and problems quickly, without second-guessing.

Determination—Willpower. Purpose. Fortitude. Grit. All of these describe a person who has not only the self-control but also the determination to succeed.

Discipline—A disciplined person lives with self-imposed limits. He or she is able to control impulses and desires.

Integrity—People of integrity follow through consistently and aim for the highest level of honesty.

Maturity—Marks of a mature person include consistent growth in common sense, wisdom, and self-control. Does this describe you?

Sacrifice—Do you give up precious time, resources, and personal preferences for the sake of others or a higher good? If so, you have the ability to sacrifice.

Steadfastness—The term "steadfast" carries with it a sense of persistent determination and loyal, unshakable commitment.

Strength—We understand physical strength, but what about inner strength? It must include moral courage; mental, emotional, and spiritual vitality; and the ability to bring about positive change.

Temperance—Are you able to restrain yourself when you are tempted to indulge? A temperate person can quietly abstain thanks to self-control.

To find out more about each of these dimensions of character and to further develop success with self-control, you are again invited to view our website at www.YourBestDestinyAssessment.com. The resources there will move you closer to godly character and to discovering God's best life for you. On page 233 of this book, you can see the questions from the assessment that measure self-control.

BECOMING YOUR BEST YOU

In what areas of your life do you struggle with self-control?

How would you define self-control?

How can self-control enhance all aspects of your personal character?

Why is it important to understand that "self" alone cannot achieve self-control?

Dear God, I confess my lack of self-control, and my need for Your sovereign control over my life. I trust in Your love and encouragement as well as Your strength, and I thank You for taking charge of my life. Amen.

7

THE PROMISE OF PERSEVERANCE

How Staying the Course Can Make You Stronger

"Mom, I need help with my math facts!" Matthew yelled as he bounced into the car.

"And my teacher wants to know if you can come in on Friday to help with reading groups," added Elijah, patting his baby sister on the head on his way to his seat.

Sara shook her head. What were two more things in the chaos her life had been recently? Working part-time. Volunteering at school, at church, and with basketball. Maintaining a house and a marriage. Taking care of three kids, one of whom demanded more of her time and energy than she felt equipped to give.

Matthew had recently been diagnosed with some special needs, finally giving Sara names for the issues they'd been having for years. She loved Matthew fiercely—yet dealing with his rages, social struggles, and learning challenges exhausted her beyond anything she'd ever known. *I need a break*, she thought, even as she knew there was no way to take a vacation from parenting.

She smiled wryly as she remembered the naive twenty-four-year-old who had jumped into motherhood expecting only warm fuzzies and compliant children. That girl wouldn't have made it five minutes with Matthew. But the woman she was now? She was less idealistic, sure, but she had the kind of strength that had developed through years of struggle. She might have fewer warm fuzzies than she had expected, but she had a better understanding of what love was really about. Some days she felt as if she were hanging on by a thread, but by the grace of God she was hanging on.

• • •

Sorrow and silence are strong, and patient endurance is godlike.

HENRY WADSWORTH LONGFELLOW

A WIFE WAS IN DESPAIR. She sat on her bed, trying to decide if she should take her son and daughter and leave her husband.

"God, I can't live this way anymore," she prayed. "I know what You've said about divorce, but I can't live in the same house with him. Help me, Lord."

It wasn't that she didn't love him. But she couldn't handle his temper. He used words like weapons, leaving her feeling crippled.

The wife was especially sensitive to her husband's anger and criticism because of her background. She was raised by a mentally ill mother who often kept her locked in a closet as a child. Her mother also told her repeatedly that she'd grow up to be a failure. The now-grown wife was starving for encouragement from her husband, not more condemnation. For so long, she'd prayed, "Change him, Lord," yet day after day it seemed her prayers went unanswered. She'd endured his harsh words for nearly fifteen years.

Hours passed as the wife sat on her bed and wrestled with the most important decision of her life: leave him and start over, or stick it out?

What would you do in her place? What would help you decide? Not sure? I'll give you a hint: It is at crisis points like these that our godly character kicks in. These are the times when our character, or lack of it, leads us to either a wrong turn or the road to God's best life for us. These are the moments when we must choose our destiny.

In this case, the wife's godly character was an invaluable guide. *Self-control* kept her from making a rash, emotional decision. *Wisdom* showed her the difficult life she and her children would face without their husband and father, including a legacy of divorce. Her strong *faith* in God reminded her that she could trust Him even though He seemed silent.

The wife took time to listen for an answer to her desperate prayer. She sensed God telling her to keep praying for changed hearts—not only her husband's, but also her own. She cried at this. The answer was painful, but it was the right one. She would not abandon her husband and her marriage. She would remain patient.

She would *persevere.*

The wife's name was Stormie Omartian, and as she prayed daily for her husband, herself, and their marriage, she at last began to see small encouragements that led to big changes. Stormie's perseverance, combined with prayer and the power of God, transformed their marriage. After forty years together, their relationship is stronger than she ever imagined it could be.[1] And because she faced and overcame those struggles, Stormie was able to write many best-selling books encouraging others about the power of prayer. She found her calling and became who she was created to be.

It was possible only because Stormie persevered.

Life in the Desert

The fifth secret to a successful life is "patient endurance," or *perseverance.* In classical Greek, perseverance is *hypomonē.* This word describes the ability of a plant to thrive in a harsh environment, literally in the deserts and on rocky slopes. Stormie had *hypomonē.* Though her marriage was in a desert, she did not give up hope that God could still bring it to life.

Men and women of strong character do not quit when difficulties occur. Instead, they patiently take on the challenges. My definition of patience is quiet perseverance. Perseverance implies more grunting and groaning than patience, but both words describe the same quality. To be patient means you don't give up. When you are provoked, you don't quit. You hang in and you persevere.

In more recent Greek and Jewish literature, *hypomonē* is used to refer to the spiritual staying power of a person's character. It is in the quiet crucible of our personal, private sufferings that our noblest dreams are born and God's greatest gifts are given. Only when people have patience, forbearance, and perseverance can they reach their God-given destiny.

We've all heard that "patience is a virtue" and that "good things come to those who wait." Many of us have been taught since we were small that our chances for success are much greater when we keep at something, when we persistently work hard at developing our knowledge and natural abilities. Few would argue with this logic.

What we may not realize or accept, however, is that the desert times in our lives—the troubles and obstacles that seem to block us—actually prepare us for and lead us to success. The Bible says, "Consider it pure joy, my brothers and sisters, whenever you face trials of many kinds, because you know that the testing of your faith produces perseverance. Let perseverance finish its work so that you may be mature and complete, not lacking anything."[2]

Our problems are not just burdens to endure but essential steps for developing one or more dimensions of our character. Often, that dimension is perseverance.

I remember a cool autumn evening when my son Wade, then nine years old, and I went rollerblading on the asphalt trail in our neighborhood. We crossed a bridge that spanned the stream flowing through our backyard, picking up speed as we coasted down an incline. For the next seven minutes, I felt as if I were floating as we wound around curves in the smooth, paved trail.

That feeling changed, however, as soon as we reached the end of the incline and turned around. Now we had to push our way back home, the coasting giving way to working. As the sweat began beading on my forehead and the ache in my legs grew, I heard Wade say, "Daddy, this is *hard*!"

"Yes, son," I said. "I know it's hard. But it's the hills that make you strong."

You don't get strong coasting downhill. The hard labor of getting through a difficult trial is like exercise. It gives your character strength and muscle. It prepares you to achieve far greater heights tomorrow than you're reaching for today.

You may have heard of a remarkable man who confronted many hills in his life. Between 1831 and 1858 he suffered two business failures, the deaths of a fiancée and a son, and a mental breakdown. This man also failed in his attempts at public office: He bid unsuccessfully for positions as state legislator, speaker of the state legislature, presidential elector, state land officer, congressional representative, US senator (twice), and US vice president.

Yet in 1860, Abraham Lincoln was elected president of the United States. He led the nation through the dark days of the Civil War, preserved the Union, and issued the Emancipation Proclamation. Many historians consider him the greatest of all US presidents.

I submit that none of Lincoln's ultimate success would have occurred had he not first learned to persevere during the difficult years that preceded his presidency. He developed empathy for the downhearted and oppressed. He turned from virtual atheism to a faith of strong conviction. He found that some ideas are worth living for—and dying for. Lincoln became one of history's most respected leaders not *in spite of* the sorrows and setbacks he endured but *because* of them.

Author Annie Dillard once wrote, "You do not have to sit outside in the dark. If, however, you want to look at the stars, darkness is necessary."[3] When you spend time in the dark, you will see and experience things that you never did in the light. And your character will grow.

Throw in the Towel?

I hope you understand and agree with what I'm saying. To achieve a level of character that begins to match God's ethos and leads to His best life for us, we must acquire a highly developed ability to persevere and to grow through our perseverance.

I can almost hear you: "Easy for you to say, Wintley. But you're not living my life. How am I supposed to persevere when I just lost my job . . . when my best friend just moved away . . . when my daughter is addicted to meth . . . when I can't imagine things ever getting better?"

I appreciate the feeling. All of us, probably more times than we'd care to admit, have felt like giving up. In those moments, we want to resign and walk away. We've become so frustrated and tired that we're at the limit of our endurance. We've given all we have, and it's getting us nowhere. So often, we decide to throw up our hands and throw in the towel.

That phrase, "throw in the towel," comes from boxing. When a boxer is too badly beaten up to continue, his coach or trainer will toss a towel into the ring to indicate the fight is over. It's something like the old signal of raising a white flag of surrender. It means "I give up." It means you've lost all hope of victory.

Recent news reports indicate that the single most occupationally frustrated group in America is church pastors. They are throwing in the towel at an alarming rate. Eventually, 40 percent of them drop out of the ministry and find another career. Before they reach that point, 75 percent of them go through a period of stress so great that they consider quitting. Incidents of mental breakdown are so high in the ministry that some insurance companies charge higher premiums for pastors than they do for employees in other businesses. Ministering to people is a stressful business. If you're not careful, it will drive you crazy.

I can relate. My first pastorate was at a wonderful little church in Sandy Springs, Maryland. For years the church grew and flourished, and everyone appeared happy. Then discord set in. Some of the strong personalities in our midst began to air their likes and dislikes in a formidable way. Anyone who works with people becomes accustomed to the noise of dissenters, but I was deeply troubled by the silence of the rest of the congregation. They knew what was going on and could have spoken up, but they didn't.

I didn't want to throw in the towel, but I also did not want to fight to remain in a situation where I wasn't wanted. Eventually, I accepted an offer to work for Alabama-based Oakwood College. Was my career as a pastor over already? I hoped not. I wasn't ready to quit on a ministry I felt God had called me to. I continued to pray about it, and to keep my eye out for opportunities. My persistence was eventually rewarded with a call from a church official. "Wintley," he said, "how would you like to become minister of our church on Capitol Hill?"

I accepted the position and enjoyed many delightful years with that church. Today, I am senior pastor of a church in Palm Bay,

Florida. Apparently, God wasn't ready for me to give up my pastoral ministry either.

As kids, my friends and I used to wrestle with each other. When you got someone pinned or in a headlock, the only way they could be freed was if they said "uncle." I don't know where that expression came from, but it means "I surrender" or "I throw in the towel." It means you've given up.

When you refuse to say "uncle" and push through the worst that the world throws at you, however, you come out on the other side with exactly what you need. According to the Bible, we are to "glory in our sufferings, because we know that suffering produces perseverance; perseverance, character; and character, hope."[4]

Does anything about this progression seem backward to you? I would expect that people who possess the gift of perseverance are able to endure hard times; that people of character are best equipped for the storms of life; that people who know how to persevere and who have character are the ones with hope.

But these words say that suffering *produces* perseverance, character, and hope. They imply that the trouble must come first, that we *need* to face conflicts and crises in order to obtain these vital qualities. Is this true?

Absolutely! This is the purpose of our problems. It's why you and I should be able to find a kind of joy in the process of working through the dilemmas and difficulties of life. Of course it's hard. Of course it hurts. Yet we can approach our trials with renewed confidence because we trust that God is at work in our situation, using it to make us more and more like Him. We don't have to give up on ourselves because He Himself is patient and will never give up on us. The longer you and I hang in there, the more we develop perseverance, strengthen our godly character, and discover hope.

A man named Drew Wills understands this. In 2004, while he was on a ski trip with his family on the slopes of Aspen, Colorado, Drew's life took a tragic turn when he spotted an out-of-control skier hurtling down the hillside toward him and tried to maneuver out of her way. Too late, he saw a pine tree in his path and slammed hard into the trunk. The impact broke his back and severed his spinal cord at the twelfth thoracic vertebra, leaving him paralyzed from the waist down.

Drew's first few days at the rehabilitation center were grim. He was used to being active and independent, but now he was bedridden and dependent on the care of others twenty-four hours a day. On top of that, he was in significant pain, feverish and vomiting; he couldn't sleep, and he developed a rash over his entire body. In short, he was a mess.

Already a devout Christian, Drew prayed as he'd never prayed before: "Please take away the pain. Please help the doctors discover what's wrong so I can get healthy and learn to function again. Please don't leave me like this."

Even in those dark days, however, Drew did not give up. He trusted that somehow God could still do something good with his life. He was grateful when the doctors finally diagnosed and treated his illness, and soon he was ready to take on the challenge of physical therapy. Most exciting was the day he learned about handcycles and other outdoor equipment designed for paraplegics. An avid cyclist, Drew realized he wouldn't have to give up his passion.

More than a year later, after working himself back into shape, he entered the 2005 Bicycle Tour of Colorado, a weeklong journey through the Rocky Mountains. Twice during the early stages of the tour, bad weather and fatigue forced him to stop before the finish line; and when he began to tire during the next leg, a 110-mile day trek, he feared he was going to come up short again.

Not wanting to feel that soul-crushing disappointment again, Drew pushed on despite the growing exhaustion in his arms. When he finally arrived at a long downhill portion that opened into a grassy mountain valley, he got his second wind and began to think, *I just might be able to do this.*

By the time he reached the final fifteen-mile stretch, he was sure of it.

If I can do this, there are all kinds of things I can do.

And he did. In 2007, Drew came in second at the Off-Road Handcycling World Championships. Two years later, he won that event and placed well in the Sadler's Alaska Challenge, widely considered the sport's most grueling race. In the years since, he has resumed his profession as an attorney, served on the board of directors for some local nonprofit organizations, and learned how to monoski and scuba dive.

Drew Wills knows firsthand about suffering that produces perseverance, character, and hope. Though he never would have asked for the accident that changed his life, it has deepened his character and drawn him closer to family, friends, and especially God.

"When you wake up every day with a reminder that certain unexpected events in life may leave you helpless and alone, even if you work hard and learn to overcome them, it's easier to depend on God," Drew says. "It's a constant reminder that He is your salvation and you have a lot to be thankful for."[5] Drew's willingness to patiently persevere has led him to become the best version of himself he can be.

Three Keys to Developing Perseverance

How about you? Are you feeling ready to tackle your next challenge with enthusiasm, knowing that the perseverance you grow will put you on the path to resembling, reflecting, and revealing the character of God? I hope so.

To help you along this journey, let me suggest three key areas of focus that will better enable you to develop the patient endurance that is perseverance. When you master them, you'll find those long-term dilemmas less daunting. More important, you'll be on your way to discovering your God-given destiny.

Learn from Each Letdown

Would-be novelist Kathryn Stockett spent a year and a half writing a manuscript. She mailed it to a literary agent. Six weeks later, she received a rejection letter that said, "Story did not sustain my interest."

Stockett didn't allow herself to get discouraged. Instead, she looked for ways to improve her manuscript. The rejections, and the rewrites, continued.

After five years and sixty manuscript rejections, Kathryn Stockett still didn't have an agent. Yet because she'd decided to learn something from each letdown and use that knowledge to improve her novel, she had a far more polished manuscript than when she'd started. She sensed that it was just a matter of time.

Her sixty-first letter struck gold. An agent named Susan Ramer offered to represent Stockett. Three weeks later, Ramer sold *The Help* to a publisher. Released in 2009, the book has since become a phenomenon, selling more than ten million copies, spending more than one hundred weeks on the *New York Times* bestseller list, and being made into a movie.

When we see someone achieving amazing success, we rarely take into account the failures they endured and the lessons they learned along the way. Thomas Edison reportedly built and tested more than one thousand lightbulbs before finally getting one to work. Michael Jordan was cut from his high school varsity basketball team. Elvis Presley, after his first performance at the Grand Ole Opry, was advised by the manager to go back to truck driving.

When you are rejected or you fall short of your goal, step back and take an objective look at the situation. Ask yourself and people you trust, "What happened here? Why didn't I succeed? What can I do differently or better next time?" Your failure today can be the fuel to lasting future success.

Sink Your Roots

In Oklahoma City, an eighty-year-old elm tree attracts tourists from all over. It is not the most remarkable tree—plenty of others are larger or greener—but this tree is valued for its perseverance. You see, the old elm survived the 1995 Oklahoma City bombing.

When Timothy McVeigh detonated his explosives at the Alfred P. Murrah Federal Building on that April morning, he killed 168 people, wounded 850, and nearly destroyed the building. The blast also stripped the branches from the elm tree and buried the trunk in debris.

As the city began to recover from the damage, few people gave any thought to the disfigured tree. No one expected it to survive. But when it began to bud, people took notice. Out of the devastation of the terrorist attack, new life now blossomed. Victims found hope in the elm's resilience, and they gave it a name: the Survivor Tree. The tree still stands today as a symbol of endurance.

That tree must have sunk its roots deep into the Oklahoma soil to survive such a deadly blast. We, too, must sink our roots deep—not in the soil but in our spiritual foundation. Unshakable faith in God is critical if we are to develop godly character, and it is essential for establishing perseverance. Without faith, we're just blindly hoping that our circumstances will turn around. Faith in God—that He has a plan for this world and for our lives, that He is actively working, that He will one day set everything right—gives our perseverance meaning.

How do we strengthen our spiritual root system? It starts with daily prayer, talking and listening to God. The Bible tells us to "always pray and never give up."[6] That should sound familiar. Even our prayer lives should reflect perseverance!

We also sink our roots deeper when we study the words of God in Scripture. The better we understand His wisdom, the better equipped we are to put it into practice when we're hit with a crisis.

Finally, we deepen our roots when we lean on family and friends who share our faith. No one expects you to endure your problems on your own. The people around you who love and care for you are invaluable resources. When you're struggling, they want to help. To help you keep from giving up, you need people who believe in you when you don't believe in yourself. Let them into your life and you'll grow deeper spiritual roots—and uncover new levels of perseverance.

Remember the Rewards That Lie Ahead

Leadership guru John Maxwell has talked about the value of patience when teaching our kids—or our employees—new tasks.

For our instruction to sink in, we have to enlist, train, direct, supervise, and redirect our children or staff. We're often tempted to give up and just take care of the work ourselves. When we do, however, we cheat ourselves over the long haul.

> Working alone is faster (at least in the beginning), but it doesn't have the same return. If you want your children to learn, grow, and reach their potential, you need to pay the price and take the time and trouble to lead them through the process—even when it means slowing down or giving up some of your agenda. It's similar with employees. Leaders aren't necessarily the first to cross the finish line—people who run alone are the fastest. Leaders are the first to bring all of their people across the finish line. The payoff to leadership—at work or home—comes on the back end.[7]

It's another way of saying that we must avoid shortcuts. The future reward will be worth the temporary trouble.

The Bible says, "Do not throw away this confident trust in the Lord. Remember the great reward it brings you! Patient endurance is what you need now, so that you will continue to do God's will. Then you will receive all that he has promised."[8]

And what has He promised? Eternal life, His constant presence, His Holy Spirit, an opportunity to participate in His Kingdom, and a love so big we can't even comprehend it. It's all a matter of perspective. Our troubles may seem big now, but the rewards will be great.

God is clear: There is a purpose for our inconveniences,

troubles, and suffering. It's true for parents and managers. It's also true for you and me. It allows us to develop the perseverance we need in order to know God's best life for us.

Possessing Patience and Perseverance

When you experience times of contrary winds and doors that are closed tightly, when you raise your voice to ask, "Why has this happened to me?"—don't give up. Your most cherished wish may have been denied, but the opposition you are facing may prove to be a blessing if you don't quit.

I have found that patience helps you handle what's going on now, while perseverance allows you to deal with a situation that doesn't let up. Patience holds you together. Perseverance keeps you going when the relief you seek is taking longer than expected. But both are vital to your character and success in life. Anything worth having—and that includes godly character as well as more tangible goals—is worth whatever effort and endurance it requires to obtain.

Yes, you will struggle as you develop a new ethos. You will make mistakes. But when you mess up, learn from your mistakes and keep going.

If you're dealing with trials or you've been overwhelmed by the wrongs of others, hold on to the strength God has given you. If you have given your life to Him, His strong Spirit lives in you. He will teach you patience and perseverance and will help you overcome your hardest trials.

Patience and perseverance build the kind of character that leads to a successful life. Never give up, and God's best life for you can be yours.

DEVELOPING PERSEVERANCE

The following are prerequisites of and beneficial qualities that result from developing patience and perseverance. Studying each will give you a better understanding of how you already reflect God's character and what you may need to develop further. They are guiding lights on the trail to your best destiny.

Cooperation—You cannot always press ahead all by yourself. Sometimes you need to collaborate with others to get things done.

Diplomacy—The art of negotiating and keeping the peace is not only for diplomats in faraway countries. It also has a place in the ordinary give-and-take of relationships.

Fellowship—When you take time to develop healthy relationships with others, you discover resources that will help you live a full and satisfying life.

Flexibility—Have you ever noticed that people of mature character are not rigidly bound to their routines? They are flexible and teachable, able to adjust to shifting circumstances without losing stability and joy.

Hospitality—Anytime you welcome others into your life, you demonstrate patient love, because people have a way of bringing unpleasant surprises with them.

Serenity—Are you calm and unruffled even when the unexpected happens? Serenity is closely related to patience.

Tact—Careful discretion with words will enable you to discuss a difficult subject without insulting or angering the other person.

Thoughtfulness—A patient person treats others with thoughtful consideration and kindness, unselfishly thinking of others' needs and desires.

Tolerance—You probably know people who reject nearly every idea they hear. A tolerant person is not narrow-minded or closed to new ways of doing things.

What have you learned from this list? Are you as patient as you thought you were? Do you possess the ability to persevere? Are these strengths or weaknesses in your character? If your answers are not what you wish they were, please don't be discouraged. After all, we've learned that a little perseverance can change your character in a big way! Take another look at our website at www.YourBestDestinyAssessment.com and see page 237 in this book for the questions on the assessment that measure perseverance. You may discover that patience and perseverance are easier to acquire than you think.

BECOMING YOUR BEST YOU

What are some synonyms for patience and perseverance?

What does it mean to say, "Quitters never win and winners never quit"?

How do you feel God is helping (or not helping) you persevere over the long haul?

Look back on a difficult time in your life. How did persevering through it affect your character?

Dear God, my prayer today is that You will supply me with much-needed patience and perseverance. Encourage me and strengthen me as I face unrelenting difficulties. Without Your help I will falter, but with You I will succeed. Amen.

8

THE GLORY OF SACREDNESS

How to Find Meaning in the Everyday

Tyson stepped back from the dishwasher, letting steam escape. How many times had he unloaded dishes so far on this shift? It was an endless cycle. Wash the dishes, dry them, put them on tables for customers to use, clear them off tables, bring them to the kitchen, and wash them again. Over and over and over, for eight hours. He needed this job, but sometimes he thought he'd die of boredom.

He lived for his days off, when he often went on a hike or biked to the park, and for his college classes, where the challenge of learning new material kept him invigorated. Outside in the sunshine or stretching his mind—now that was where he felt a sense of meaning, even a sense of God's presence. But here at his mundane job? How could he find purpose in washing dishes?

He grabbed the clean silverware and started wrapping sets in cloth napkins, stopping to toss a stained napkin back into the laundry bin. Maybe part of it was just doing his job the best he could or being kind to the people around him. Maybe another part of it was trying to believe the crazy truth that even here—in the midst of suds and steam and broken dishes, in the most boring parts of his day—life had purpose. God was present.

• • •

How little people know who think that holiness is dull.
When one meets the real thing . . . it is irresistible.

C. S. LEWIS

We live in an irreverent time. One can hardly watch a movie, pick up a novel, listen to the radio, or talk to a neighbor without hearing profanity and God's name taken in vain. The sacred, it seems, has been virtually expunged from our vocabularies and drained from our lives. Sadly, this irreverence extends beyond our entertainment and casual conversation. Each day, our ears and eyes drink in what is disrespectful and profane. Many no longer see our existence as a sacred gift from God.

According to *Merriam-Webster's*, the word *profane* means "to treat (something sacred) with abuse, irreverence, or contempt." Think about that for a moment. It means to take something sacred and reduce it to a status that is base and common. To profane something means to bring it low, down to the gutter.

That might be how a pastor once felt after he pulled into a country gas station while on vacation. As the attendant filled the car with gas, he happened to look at the vehicle's tires.

"You know," the man said, "I think you oughta know that your [blankety-blank] tire is about to blow. If it does, you and your family will have a wreck. I think if I were you, I'd get a new tire."

The pastor agreed to this, and the man set to work. He also talked as he worked, filling in nearly every other word with a curse, most of them invoking God's name.

The pastor finally couldn't take it anymore. He looked at the man and said, "Sir, I don't want God to damn my car. I wish you wouldn't say that."

The attendant was startled. "Oh," he said. "I'm sorry I offended you."

"You know, sir," the pastor said, "you work with tires, and you spared my family from an accident and possible disaster—and I'm grateful. But I'm a pastor. I work with souls. And when I heard you talking like that, I thought, *He spared my family from disaster; I want to spare him from disaster.* So you need to hear me when I say that using God's name in vain is a very, very expensive thing to do. You can't use the Lord's name in vain and not pay a price."[1]

That pastor was right. We all pay a price when we take what is sacred and turn it into what is profane. God clearly warns us of the consequences in one of His Ten Commandments: "You must not misuse the name of the LORD your God. The LORD will not let you go unpunished if you misuse his name."[2] When we treat the name of our Creator with anything less than reverence, it's as if we are denying His power and holiness. It is a way of trying to drag God down to our level.

The struggle to tame our tongues indicates another problem, one within our souls. It means our ethos is not what it should be. It is a sign that our character lacks a holy quality. When we speak or even think in a way that degrades God, it shows that we have lost our reverence for what is holy.

And what is the cost of this profane attitude? It is the steady erosion of our ethos. Perhaps without us even noticing it, our faith in God and belief in our ability to fulfill our best destiny shrinks. When we forget how holy, powerful, and awe-inspiring God is, we lose ground on the other pillars of God's ethos. We find it just a little easier to compromise our moral standards, lose control, or give up when we should instead persevere. It might mean lingering too long on racy images that pop up on a website, shouting at the kids, or no longer trying to communicate in a marriage. Pretty soon a minor issue turns into a major problem. Our faith, our relationships, our careers, and our marriages suffer. Our dreams of becoming our best selves seem a distant memory.

What is the solution to disrespect toward our lives and our Lord? Simply put, we need to renew our sense of the sacred.

Holiness in Hidden Places

In the middle of winter, a young Frenchman named Nicolas Herman once examined a leafless tree. Herman felt as dead as the tree appeared to be, yet he knew that in springtime the tree would bloom into abundance once more. As Herman meditated on this, he felt a new and startling love for God. He began to nurture the hope that God would bring him, like the tree, life and fullness with a change in season.

Nicolas Herman joined a monastery and took the name Brother Lawrence. He was assigned to cook and clean in the monastery kitchen. As he performed the most mundane of tasks, he dedicated each moment to God. He found holiness in everyday living: "It is enough for me to pick up but a straw from the ground for the love of God."[3] Brother Lawrence lived with a sense of the sacred—a sense of the constant holy presence of God.

How about it—do you honor what is holy as you move through the routine of your day? Are you able to see the sacred mystery in the mundane occurrences of traffic jams, grocery-store lines, TV commercials, and taking out the trash? Do you discover holiness not just at church but also in the hidden places of your life?

Author Nancy Jo Sullivan made just such a discovery while Christmas shopping in a department store. She'd recently moved into a new home, and after the bustle of unpacking boxes, baking holiday cookies, and wrapping presents, she barely had enough energy to keep her eyes open.

As she shopped, she noticed the Salvation Army bell ringer

near the entrance to the store—an old man with white hair and a wrinkled face, but the energy of a much younger man. He was ringing his bell and dancing around the red collection pot while he sang to the departing customers: "Joy to the world, the Lord is come."

A woman wearing a Christmas-tree sweater hurried past the bell ringer, frowning and carrying several shopping bags.

"No joy for the Lord?" the man called to her.

The woman ignored him and rushed on. Nancy Jo understood the feeling as more shoppers passed the singing volunteer, more focused on managing their bags of presents than on anything else.

Then something wonderful happened:

> As busy shoppers made a wide perimeter around the bell ringer, an old woman, her back hunched and her gait slow, approached him. She smiled as she clicked open a tattered purse and dropped four quarters into the slotted red pail.
>
> The man took off his ear-muffed hat and bowed to her. "May I have this dance?" he asked. The woman blushed and began to giggle. As she drew herself up, her wrinkles seemed to fade. The two of them began to shuffle around the store entry, the old man gently guiding the frail woman in graceful glides and turns.
>
> "Joy to the world . . . the Savior reigns . . ." their voices rang out in happy unison.[4]

As Nancy Jo watched, she found herself wanting to join in the department store waltz. There was something uplifting about their dance, something that rose above the stress of the season. For a few wonderful seconds, these two connected with each other in a way that honored God.

It was, in an unexpected place and time, a holy moment.

We're a lot like the other shoppers in the story above—too preoccupied with our routine duties, too exhausted to keep our eyes open long enough to see the God moments around us. How can we rediscover what we might call everyday holiness? How do we develop an affinity for sacredness that enables us to resemble, reflect, and reveal the character of God?

We can begin by taking inventory of what we hold as holy. What is it that moves you toward a reverence for the spiritual, toward an awareness of the divine that exists both within and beyond this life? Is it prayer? Worship? Church services? Reading the Bible? Music? A walk along ocean waves on a deserted beach? The sound of soft footsteps just before your four-year-old jumps into bed with you on a Saturday morning?

For me, it begins with a focus on God's supremacy. I was sixteen when I first embraced the sacredness of what the theologian Athanasius called the *prima veritas* or "first truth"—that God is the most powerful force and personality in the universe.

I believe that He is the great Creator, the one who made the heavens and the earth, and that by His power the path of every planet in the heavens was established. I believe that every act of divine intelligence and every evidence of rhythm, rule, and order—the steady precision of the stars, the constant rotation of the earth, and its never-failing orbit around the sun—is the work of His hands. I believe that everything in nature is a mighty witness to the dominion of God, who created both the soil and the seed and taught them to work together.

I believe that God *is* sacredness, the reason that angels proclaim,

"Holy, holy, holy is the LORD Almighty; the whole earth is full of his glory."[5] No one can match the sacred essence of God. As we have already seen, we usually fall woefully short.

And yet He calls us to the sacred: "But now you must be holy in everything you do, just as God who chose you is holy. For the Scriptures say, 'You must be holy because I am holy.'"[6] God is pure, blameless, and set apart from any other being in the universe. He desires that we develop a holy character, one that grows more and more like His. We also need to acquire a sense of the sacred—an understanding that because of God's presence in the world, even the ordinary can take on significant spiritual meaning.

What do you hold as holy? What stops you in mid-step or mid-thought because it suddenly strikes you as sacred? What do you regard as worthy of reverence? These are the things that should inspire awe, meaning, and holy moments in your life. They are also what move you closer to God's best life for you.

Let's take a look at a few possibilities.

Our Lives Are Sacred

God created human beings in His own image. We are like Him. So when we come across another person, even if it's a homeless man in an alley or the coworker who made us look bad in front of the boss, we are seeing a reflection—however distorted—of supreme holiness. That should inspire a different attitude in us toward our fellow men and women.

Abraham Heschel, an American rabbi and Jewish theologian, said: "The awe that we sense or ought to sense when standing in the presence of a human being is a moment of intuition for the likeness of God which is concealed in his essence. . . . Something sacred is at stake in every moment."[7]

I recently learned a very compelling and personal lesson about the sacredness of our lives from one of my aunts, whom I hadn't seen in more than ten years. When she visited me recently, she told me a story that brought tears to my eyes.

Two years before I was born, my aunt's sister Pearl (who was also my father's sister) died while having an abortion. This was in 1953. When my mother, Elaine, became pregnant with me, some people counseled her to have an abortion. But because of the grief and pain the family had gone through in losing Pearl, my father's sisters became a unified force to make sure that history would not repeat itself and that the child Elaine was bearing would live.

Moreover, before I was born, my two grandmothers made a pact with one another that they would pray for this child's life to be a blessing to the world. My aunt told me she often saw her mother standing over my bassinet with a candle, praying, "Lord, make this child's life a blessing to the world."

God answered my grandmothers' prayers and gave me a voice unique in the world, as well as a heart and a determination to be a blessing to others. Little did I know that my life would become an answer to my grandmothers' prayers. But what moved me most profoundly was the realization that I was able to live because my Aunt Pearl had died. In a sense, she had given her life for me.

Even without knowing that story until very recently, after all the drama of my childhood, I desperately wanted to become the best man I could be, a spiritual man and a man of honor, a man who lives by the eight pillars of a godly ethos: faith, virtue, wisdom, self-control, perseverance, sacredness, kindness, and love. By God's grace and power, I have pursued His best life for me and my best destiny.

Our Bodies Are Sacred

Our bodies are holy not only because they contain the sacred life that God has given us but also because they serve as a sanctuary for the Holy Spirit once we invite Him into our lives. The apostle Paul wrote, "Don't you know that you yourselves are God's temple and that God's Spirit dwells in your midst? If anyone destroys God's temple, God will destroy that person; for God's temple is sacred, and you together are that temple."[8]

Friendship with God Is Sacred

Picture your best friend. I'll bet that relationship is so special to you that it seems almost sacred. What have you done over the years to nurture that friendship? Shared good times? Mailed birthday cards? Cried over coffee? Revealed the secrets of your heart?

What I bet you haven't done is continually curse your friend in front of others. The sacred and the profane are incompatible. They cannot reside together. God wants our relationship with Him to be the most real, most important friendship in our lives. Yet only when we see ourselves as called to be holy can we imagine an intimate friendship with God. Then we must treat that friendship as the sacred treasure it is, honoring and respecting our relationship with the Lord in everything we do and say.

The Work and Will of God Are Sacred

When we enter into the work and will of God, we tread on sacred ground. Everything we do takes on new significance. We are operating on the God level.

If we were working for the government on a special project, we would have to pass through certain clearances to ensure our trustworthiness. When we work on God's special projects on earth, He requires that we be cleansed—by confessing our sin and receiving His forgiveness—and that we respect the sacred nature of our work. The Bible tells us, "Touch no unclean thing! Come out from it and be pure, you who carry the articles of the LORD's house."[9]

You may tell a friend about how much God means to you, but if she sees you more focused on acquiring a new car or new kitchen than on pleasing Him, your words will carry little weight. It is when you bring a sense of reverence to fulfilling God's work and will that your efforts will have lasting impact.

Truth Is Sacred

By its very nature, truth is sacred. It is the highest bar that can be set on reality. Without it, humankind would drift hopelessly along, never knowing if it was going or coming. Deep inside we all know this. It's the reason we all seek truth in some form.

When we lie about why we were late to the meeting or about how we spent someone's check, we pollute the truth. Our God-given conscience tells us that we have done wrong. We feel off-center and somehow lessened. On the other hand, when we embrace truth, regardless of the consequences, a corresponding positive emotion wells up inside us. Our hearts recognize truth and cling to it.

God is truth in its ultimate, sacred form. This is why David writes in one of his psalms, "You want complete honesty, so teach me true wisdom."[10]

The Name of God Is Sacred

Imagine that you have a friend who works in the movie industry and has arranged for you to attend a movie premiere. When you arrive at the theater, you must mention your friend's name to gain admittance. But what if you show up and begin to shout insults about your friend? Chances are you won't get in after all.

As we have already discussed, it is commonplace today to hear God's name used as a profanity, as a response to surprise, or in any of a dozen other irreverent ways. Each time we deny the sacred nature of God's name, we diminish its effectiveness in our lives. God's name is backed by His immeasurable power and person. Nothing we do or say can change that in the least. But when we trivialize the sacred nature of God's name, we also begin to trivialize our view of Him. We have a weakened sense of His power, presence, and holiness, and that deeply affects how we live.

I heard of a man on a New York subway who was deeply grieved by the way some young men were cursing and defaming the name of God. After about ten minutes of this, he walked up to the young men and said, "I wish you wouldn't curse using that name. You're talking about my very best friend."

Marriage Is Sacred

God encourages us to enter into covenant relationships with each other as well, and to do this with similar respect and consideration. We recognize the sacred nature of marriage by taking a vow and pledging our fidelity to our spouse.

If we vigilantly guard our marriage relationships, we will find that great benefits will come our way, for a good marriage is second only to a good relationship with God. When our marriages model a thriving relationship with Him, we find not only love, comfort, support, encouragement, and physical fulfillment but also a sense of the sacred.

Our Free Will Is Sacred

If there is one thing I believe for sure, it is that God recognizes as sacred the right of every human being to choose to live according to what they believe—whether right or wrong. Unless we are violating the rights of others, God considers our free will a most sacred right, and one that He will not violate. Instead of making us obedient robots, He chose to create us in His image and to give us the gift of free will. Then, instead of revoking that right when we abused it, God chose to shoulder the responsibility Himself for our misuse of our freedom. Rather than take away our right to choose our destiny, God assumed all liability for our mistakes, should we repent of them and ask forgiveness.

God not only considers our free will sacred and inviolate, He sees it as an indispensable prerequisite to the development of our character. And He has promised to reward those who strive to resemble, reflect, and reveal His character.

God's Spirit Is Sacred

All these things, however, are secondary to the sacredness of the Holy Spirit. The Holy Spirit is the third element of the Trinity—God the Father, Jesus the Son, and the Spirit. One of the great and wonderful mysteries of faith is that each is an individual Person with emotions and a will, yet each is part of the one God.

The Holy Spirit lives within the believer—it is through His Spirit that God is able to be with us everywhere and for every moment of every day. He is the comforter, communicator, and purveyor of God's power in our lives. The Holy Spirit is sacred by His very nature. It is impossible to enter or sustain relationship with God without Him.

There is nothing more sacred to me than the sense of God's presence in my life and the understanding that His Spirit dwells within me. Without Him, the development of character in my life and yours is doomed. Without Him, we will never fulfill our supreme destiny. But with His sacred presence inside us, our possibilities are endless. Nothing is impossible for those who treasure the presence of God in their lives—nothing!

I am grateful for my wife, my children, and my health. I thank God for many true and faithful friends and benefactors whom I can never repay. They are all precious in my eyes. I am grateful for all those who have helped me through their prayers and example. I'm grateful for miracles I've seen that border on the spectacular and blessings that are often hidden from my view. I'm grateful for favors long forgotten and for the care and generosity of kind faces. But nothing can compare to the presence of God's Spirit in my life. My determination to hold on to God's Spirit does far more to define my ethos than anything else.

When I evaluate my life right now, I see that I may not have everything I want. Yet with God's Spirit inside me, I have all that I could ever need and much more than I deserve. His Spirit gives me boldness and confidence as I come before God with my prayers and requests. God's goodness toward me has been boundless and all-encompassing.

If you aren't sure if you have God's Holy Spirit inside you, I encourage you to invite Him into your life right now. Tell Him about the mistakes you've made and give them to Him, asking for His forgiveness. Tell Him that you believe in Him and want to follow His path for your life. Hold nothing back in your mind and heart. You will discover not only a new sense of the sacred but also a relationship that will transform you, taking you into God's best life for you—and into eternity.

Activate the Sacred

When we remind ourselves of what we hold as holy and begin to cherish these gifts from God, we begin to see the sacred all around us. Sights and sounds that we ignored before suddenly take on meaning. Perhaps for the first time, we appreciate God's holy presence.

Yet to develop a character that begins to resemble the holiness of God, we must do more. We must *activate* the sacred and incorporate it into our daily lives.

Years ago, when I attended Oakwood College, I had the opportunity to hear Dr. E. E. Cleveland speak in our gym. I was eager to learn from this well-known preacher, author, and civil-rights activist. I watched Dr. Cleveland while another speaker introduced him. He sat with his eyes closed and his chin resting on his hand. His body swayed slightly as if he was in a trance, and his feet tapped the floor in an unusual cadence. It was the most captivating pre-speech ritual I'd ever seen.

I was even more captivated, however, by Dr. Cleveland's talk. Never had I heard such a powerful speaker. I was awestruck. So was everyone else—the overcrowded gymnasium was so quiet when he was through, we could have heard a mouse squeak.

What gave this man such power to move human hearts? I realized it had to do with his pre-speech practice. Apparently, before every speaking appearance, Dr. Cleveland pleaded with God for power to present his words effectively. He made a holy connection that infused a sense of the sacred into every syllable.

From that night forward I adopted Dr. Cleveland's habit of praying before speaking or singing. I've learned to agonize and long for the presence of God to be felt in my discourse or song. When someone introduces me to an audience, I sit with my chin in my hands, eyes closed and body swaying, while I pray for the Holy Spirit to use me and whatever talent the Lord has given me.

When I stand to sing, it is as if I can feel a wind at my back. God Himself takes charge of my voice. Because I have activated the sacred, I enter a holy realm. The impact on not just me but also on the audience is profound.

Never be afraid to ask for and acknowledge God's presence, even if you're worried about how it will be received. I have tried to take this philosophy to heart. In 1984, I sang "God Uses Ordinary People" immediately after presidential candidate Jesse Jackson's stirring keynote address at the Democratic National Convention. Many try to separate faith from politics, and I did not know how people would react to a spiritual song in that setting. Yet I watched as the convention delegates and audience joined hands and swayed to the music. It was as if we were having an old-fashioned tent revival in the middle of a political rally. Even better, CBS news anchor Dan Rather interrupted his analysis of Jackson's speech to hear me sing. Fifty million viewers listened as the sacred entered their living rooms.

When I was invited to sing on the popular TV programs *Saturday Night Live* and *Soul Train,* I wondered what hip audiences would think of a gospel-singing preacher. But I didn't change my approach at all, and both audiences treated me with warmth and respect.

The same thing happened years later when I sang for a very different audience. I joined Chuck Colson, the former Watergate conspirator who became an influential Christian and founded the ministry Prison Fellowship, in a visit to a men's prison in Marion County, Florida. When I began to hum "Amazing Grace," all the prisoners, without prompting, got out of their chairs and stood at attention. Something in the words and melody stirred a powerful response in those men. It was an unexpected, holy moment.

When your character begins to resemble and reflect God's sacred character, He will use you to reveal that character to others. I believe this may be what happened the day I sensed God nudging me to send a note to US President Bill Clinton. I have been friends with Bill Clinton since 1990, when we met at a function in Alabama where I sang. He was the governor of Arkansas, but I mistakenly believed he was governor of Alabama—a faux pas he's never let me forget.

Years later, after he became president, the Monica Lewinsky sex scandal erupted. This was when I sensed God encouraging me to contact the president. I felt I was supposed to encourage President Clinton to read Psalm 69, which is both a plea by King David for God to have mercy and save him from enemies and also a confession of sin. In a note to the president, I urged him to read the psalm.

I learned later that during a heated discussion among his cabinet members about the effects of the scandal, the president read aloud from this psalm. Then he retired to his room and wrote the speech where he first admitted his transgressions to the American public. President Clinton invited me to the White House to be present when he delivered that speech. As I sat there and listened, I was amazed to think that God had used me—along with many others, no doubt—to prompt the president to confess his mistakes.

God uses each of us for His holy purposes when our character begins to reflect His own glorious sacredness. He invites you to sense the sacred—to be aware of His presence—throughout your life. When we're aware of God's presence in our lives and our world, we are better able to see through His eyes and with His perspective. Our eyes are open to see how He is working and how we might be a part of it, giving us a sense of significance and purpose. And when we're constantly aware of His presence with us, we'll see a change in how we use our time and what is important to us. His holiness will infuse us.

It may be an extraordinary moment—a sunset, an award-acceptance speech, or a marriage proposal. It may be far more mundane—waiting for a bus in the rain or brushing your teeth at night. The holy is not limited to what is "spiritually correct." God is with us and is working in our world, no matter what we do and no matter where we go. As we celebrate the sacred and make it an integral piece of our ethos, we dive that much deeper into God's best life for us.

A SPIRIT OF SACREDNESS

The English word *sacred* means "holy" or "deserving to be held in highest esteem and protected from violation or encroachment." The following list of prerequisites for and by-products of sacredness should help you determine the strength of your commitment to what is holy and godly.

Adoration—Genuine adoration goes beyond merely admiring someone. It leads us into both honor and worship.

Awe—Anything that inspires awe combines a sense of the wonderful and the terrible. We respond with a wondering reverence tinged with fear.

Holiness—You've heard that cleanliness is next to godliness? Holiness is too. A truly holy person displays a noticeable sanctity and piety, a supernaturally natural godliness that surpasses any smug imitation.

Humility—There is nothing holy about arrogance, pride, or aggressiveness. A person whose character reflects the sacred is modest, unpretentious, and deferential.

Piety—Only those who are particularly devoted to the divine or to worship earn the title of "pious." Their respect for the sacred separates them from the profane.

Respect—Who makes you sit up straighter when he walks in the room or listen more closely when she speaks? These are signs that you highly regard a person and consider him or her worthy of respect.

Reverence—You can appreciate something that is sacred even without thoroughly understanding why it is sacred. Respect, admiration, deference, awe, love, and even worship are intermingled in a reverent attitude.

Righteousness—The "default setting" of a righteous person is to conform to God's will. Such a person has a very strong sense of the sacred and awareness of right versus wrong.

Truth—A person who stands for truth represents integrity, trustworthiness, candor, and fidelity to what is right and good.

As before, you can further explore these qualities and how they relate to a character of sacredness by viewing our website at www.YourBestDestinyAssessment.com. On page 241 of this book, you can see the questions from the assessment that measure your sensitivity to sacredness.

Our attitude toward what is sacred cannot be easily hidden because it will constantly be reflected in our words and actions. If we have a reverent attitude toward God, others will know almost immediately. If we do not, they will see that as well. Respect for the sacred is deeply internal, yet it will greatly affect everything and everyone in our world—our relationships, opportunities, accomplishments, hopes, dreams, and most of all, our best destiny.

BECOMING YOUR BEST YOU

How would you define the word *sacred*?

What is your attitude toward what is sacred?

How does your relationship with God affect your attitude toward the sacred?

What are some ways your life might change as you begin to show more honor and respect for God's presence?

Dear God, thank You for giving me the magnificent gift of choice. It is my desire to honor You in everything I do and say and to esteem You properly in my life. Give me a deep heart understanding of the things that are sacred in my life so that I might please You at all times. Amen.

9

THE PRACTICE OF KINDNESS

How to Make Every Relationship in Your Life Better

Mark left the conference room, feeling frustrated. Once again he'd told his team that he needed help to meet a project deadline, and once again there had been an awkward silence until finally the newest hire had reluctantly volunteered, apparently resigning herself to her status as lowest on the totem pole. Why was it so hard to get anyone to step up? He wanted to create more of a team atmosphere—all for one and one for all, that kind of thing—but it was harder than he'd expected. He hardly knew these people. How was he supposed to get them to work together?

As Mark headed back to his desk, he bumped into the HR assistant. "Oh, hi, Mark," she said. "I was just about to drop this off for you. It's a list of your employees' birthdays." She smiled at his blank look as he reached out to take the paper. "You know, in case you want to give them a card or take them out to lunch or something." She shrugged. "It doesn't have to be big. Sometimes people just want to be noticed."

As she walked down the hall, Mark looked down at the paper in his hand. Could improving his team's morale really be that simple? Could little acts of kindness make that much of a difference?

. . .

Kindness is the language which the deaf
can hear and the blind can see.

MARK TWAIN

On a warm summer evening, a group of friends sat on the back patio of a Washington, DC, home, where they were enjoying a feast of marinated steaks and jumbo shrimp. Suddenly, a hooded man slid in through an open gate and put the barrel of a handgun to the head of a fourteen-year-old guest.

"Give me your money or I'll start shooting," he said.

The five adult friends, including the girl's parents, froze in fear. Tragedy was only a finger twitch away.

Finally, one of the guests spoke. Her response changed the tense situation dramatically.

"We were just finishing dinner," the woman, named Cristina, said. "Why don't you have a glass of wine with us?"

The statement seemed to disarm the intruder. He indeed took a sip. "That's good wine," he said.

The father of the girl with the gun to her head invited the intruder to take the whole glass. Cristina offered him the bottle. The would-be robber, his hood down now, took another sip and ate a bite of cheese that was on the table.

Then he tucked the gun into the pocket of his nylon sweatpants. "I think I may have come to the wrong house," he said. "I'm sorry."

Already surprised by the man's change in attitude, the group was shocked by his next comment: "Can I get a hug?"

Cristina didn't hesitate. She stood and wrapped her arms around the stranger. Then it was the girl's father's turn, followed by the mother of the formerly threatened girl. The two other adult guests also gave him a squeeze.

The intruder had a final request: "Can we have a group hug?"

The five adults surrounded him, arms out.

To the relief of everyone, the man then walked away. Nothing was stolen, and no one was hurt.[1]

Such is the power of the practice of kindness.

For most of our history, we humans have recognized and accepted the potential and the benefits of this power. Kindness is, after all, a cornerstone of most of the world's religions. It has also been admired by many of history's great thinkers. In the first century, the Stoic philosopher Seneca stated that "no one can live a happy life if he turns everything to his own purposes. Live for others if you want to live for yourself."[2] In the next century, the Roman emperor and philosopher Marcus Aurelius counseled, "A man's true delight is to do the things he was made for. He was made to show goodwill to his kind."[3]

Like so many of our best character qualities, however, kindness seems to have fallen out of favor in modern times. We tend to dismiss people who are publicly kind as attention seekers, sentimentalists, or hypocrites. Genuine generous deeds are so rare that, when they do occur, they make front-page headlines.

All too often today, kindness draws not our admiration but our suspicion and scorn. School districts across the country have suspended students for giving a hug to fellow students. Recently, a male Colorado student was suspended and initially accused of sexual harassment for kissing a fellow student on her cheek. The suspended student was six years old.[4]

Society seems to be telling us, "Forget about being nice to each other; just focus on yourself." The message is that we won't be able to succeed in our careers or get ahead in life unless our priority is taking care of number one.

That message has gotten through. Baby Boomers were labeled the "Me Generation" in the 1970s. Millennials—people born between the early 1980s and the early 2000s—have been described as the "Me Me Me Generation." Whatever the terms, selfishness seems to be rampant in our society, while kindness has been thrown out with the trash.

Maybe this is what the poet e. e. cummings was talking about when he wrote, "Pity this busy monster, manunkind."[5] Not mankind, but man *un*kind. Sadly, his description seems all too accurate. As we move through our lives intently focused on our own needs, we repeatedly miss opportunities to demonstrate compassion to those around us. Just as significantly, we also miss the benefit to ourselves.

Kindness has become almost a hidden pleasure. Basic courtesy may still be practiced, but few people stretch that into genuine kindness, especially when it involves people they don't know or who may not be able to reciprocate. Sometimes we seem nearly ashamed of our compassion, as if it were a foolish indulgence.

As we will see, however, God has an entirely different view.

Doing to Others

Benevolence . . . brotherly affection . . . compassion . . . kindness. Some may mistakenly identify this trait with a warm, fuzzy feeling, something like our mood after a relaxing session in the hot tub or stroll in the park. But kindness is not about how you or I feel. It is an active element of our character, one that seeks out ways to help others.

One of the most remarkable teachings of Jesus is this statement: "Do to others whatever you would like them to do to you. This is the essence of all that is taught in the law and the prophets."[6] I believe the emphasis should be on the first word of that declaration: *do.*

We refer to this maxim today as the Golden Rule. It is, as Jesus said, the essence or core of God's instruction to us. It is what our behavior should look like when we relate to others.

The Bible is filled with examples of God's kindness toward you and me, His children. He offers us the beauty of His creation—scenic sunrises and sunsets, colorful butterflies, and the majesty of the constellations. He provides food and makes it pleasurable for us to eat (after all, He could have made it all taste like dirt!). He provides families and opportunities for friendship and fellowship. He forgives when we confess our mistakes after doing wrong. He grants us the gift of life itself.

Nothing more clearly states the case for God's compassionate character, however, than the life, death, and resurrection of Jesus. By allowing His Son to be unjustly nailed to a wooden cross and killed so that each of us can enjoy living forever in heaven with Him, God shows that life-altering kindness is the essence of His ethos. This is why He desires that we adopt it as our character as well. Kindness is more than simply an agreeable attitude. It has the power to transform us and everyone we come in contact with.

I encountered an example of this type of kindness during my college years. In those days, I helped earn tuition money by doing weekend concerts. On one of those weekends, the concert ran late and I missed my return flight to Huntsville, Alabama. I finally found another flight that would take me through Atlanta and then home. The first leg of the trip was uneventful, but after I landed in Atlanta, an airline official told me I needed another fifty-five dollars to pay for my last flight home.

I didn't have fifty-five dollars. I didn't have a checkbook or a credit card. The concert organizers had paid me fifty dollars for singing. That and a thin dime in my pocket was all I carried.

One look into the airline official's cold blue eyes told me I had no hope of talking myself out of this situation. No protests or explanations would carry any weight with this businesslike woman. Slowly I reached into my pocket, pulled out my money, and placed it on the counter.

"Is that all the money you have?" she asked.

"That's all." It was now almost midnight. My poor brain was too weary to try to work out a solution to what seemed an unsolvable problem.

The official worked her figures again and looked at me. She wrinkled her brow in consternation. It seemed as if she was asking herself what she should do. Should she leave me stranded in Atlanta or should she bend the rules and let this college student through without paying the full fare? With downcast eyes, I waited and prayed. When I looked at her face again, I saw that her decision was made.

"I am sorry," she said firmly. "I must have the full fare. I can't give you any of the company's money."

My heart sank.

"But," she continued crisply, "I can give you some of my own money."

She reached under the counter, took a five-dollar bill out of her purse, and put it alongside my money. Then she quickly wrote out a new ticket and handed it and the dime to me. It was a wonderful and unexpected gesture that left me speechless with gratitude.

Then there was the woman who once opened her home to me. I was still in high school, on tour as a soloist with a college choir.

We sang at a church in the small town of Munising, Michigan, which even today has a population of less than 2,500 people.

After our performance, one of our hosts announced that, since our choir was so large, the community didn't have enough places for us to stay that night. When they asked for additional volunteer hosts, a woman named Betty Rohac said she and her family would take a student—provided it was me! Something about my singing had inspired Betty. I deeply appreciated her kindness and encouraging words.

A few years later, I had the opportunity to extend a bit of kindness myself. I sang at an event at the Baltimore Civic Center. After my performance, a young woman approached me. I recognized her as the host of a local television talk show. "I feel as if I can talk to you," she said. "Would you be able to spare a few minutes?"

The woman seemed sincere. I invited her to visit my wife and me at our home. When she came, she explained that she was concerned about her future and career. We talked, shared, and prayed. Later, I sensed God speaking to me about this young woman. I said to her, "God has impressed me to tell you that He's going to bless you and give you an opportunity to speak to millions of people."

"Do you really think so, Wintley?" she said. "Do you think God would do that for me?"

I assured her I believed it. It was a small thing, but I was pleased that God seemed to be using me to encourage this young lady's dreams.

Compassion in action—what the world sometimes refers to as random acts of kindness—has an immediate impact on both the receiver and giver. The beneficiary feels valued, reassured, and uplifted. When someone contributes to another's sense of self-worth and self-esteem, he or she gives more than money can buy.

What is surprising, perhaps, is that the giver benefits just as much. When we are kind to others, it renews our sense of connection to our fellow humans. We gain a sudden injection of encouragement. We are left feeling just a bit more optimistic about ourselves and our collective futures.

What we're about to see, however, is that kindness toward others does more than create short-term positive feelings. It has a lasting impact that leads to long-term success . . . and, eventually, to our best destiny.

Succeeding through Kindness

When the topic is keys to succeeding in business, kindness is not usually the first thought that comes to people's minds. The perception of kind leaders is that they are either too timid to be truly effective or that they rely on being "nice" because they lack courage, toughness, or persuasion.

What experts are discovering, however, is that practicing kindness actually brings about business success. Authors William F. Baker and Michael O'Malley recently interviewed executives and business leaders from around the world and discussed the results in their book, *Leading with Kindness*. They wrote, "Most of the leaders we spoke with invoked the Golden Rule as their management philosophy, noting that adherence to this principle is the surest way to build close-knit, high-performing communities."[7]

Bosses like these don't remain holed up in their offices. Instead, they take the time to connect with employees, offering a kind word when appropriate: "Sharon, your presentation was right on target. The statistics you included backed up your point perfectly"; or "Dave, I saw how you took care of that unhappy customer.

I appreciate how you listened to him tell the whole story and patiently explained what his options were."[8]

When possible, these leaders show a genuine interest in the personal lives of their staff and offer encouragement when they hear about problems both in the office and at home. These simple, genuine expressions of kindness leave their team members feeling valued. The result is not only a better working environment in the short term, but also a team of employees who remain loyal to the company and are motivated to do their best work over the long term. Success and company profits are almost guaranteed to follow.

When businesses extend the same kind attitude toward their customers, both sides again come out as winners. A few years ago, for example, Amazon replaced a five-hundred-dollar video game ordered by a father for his son. The fault was not Amazon's—a neighbor had signed for the video game but it disappeared, apparently stolen, from an apartment building hallway before it reached its final destination. When the father called a customer service representative to explain, he feared a hassle at best and a harsh "tough luck" at worst. Instead, however, the service representative promptly shipped off a new video game at no charge. Even the additional shipping was free.

The father was thrilled with the kindness demonstrated by the company. You would figure, though, that it wasn't nearly as good a deal for Amazon. The firm was out five hundred dollars plus the cost of the additional shipping.

What Amazon didn't know, however, was that the father was also a business columnist for the *New York Times*. He wrote about his positive experience in an article sent to thousands of readers across the country, resulting in publicity worth many times the cost of a single video game.[9]

When we show even a little bit of compassion, empathy, or thoughtfulness toward another person, it's as if we drop a pebble into a pond. The ripples in the water keep going and going, creating an impact far beyond what we imagine. Sometimes they even hit the opposite shore and bounce all the way back to us.

That's certainly been true in my life. Remember the airline official who chipped in five dollars so I could buy a ticket home? Her name was Pat Pullen, and her unexpected gesture marked the beginning of a friendship that continued for the rest of her life. Over the next few years, I made many stops at the Atlanta airport. Whenever I could, which was several times a month, I looked for Pat. We became like family.

Pat shared all the major developments of my life. When I graduated from Oakwood College, she rejoiced at my moment of triumph. When I got married, Pat was eager to meet my new bride. When I made my first album, Pat was one of the first to receive a copy. When we traveled on her airline soon after our first baby was born, Pat held our new son tenderly and admired him as if he were her own.

One day at the airport, Pat let me know that she'd been diagnosed with Hodgkin's disease. The next few years were difficult for Pat as she struggled with that form of cancer. I encouraged her whenever I could, and I know she appreciated my friendship and support.

Pat is gone now, yet today I look back so fondly on those years and our surprising relationship. Her impulsive, generous act at the moment of a college student's desperate need was the catalyst to a wonderful, rewarding connection that neither of us would ever have imagined.

I feel the same way about Betty Rohac. I enjoyed my time with the Rohacs so much after that first home stay that we kept in touch. I became a regular visitor to the family home in tiny Munising. On Lake Superior, they even taught me how to waterski. (The water is so cold there, you're motivated to learn fast so you don't fall in!)

Betty became a surrogate mother to me; she seemed to think of me almost as a son. She provided funds to help me get started in college, and astonishingly to me, she donated ten thousand dollars toward the cost of my first album. I think she took great pleasure in following my career and life. Though she, too, is gone now, I deeply treasure the memory of our friendship.

Then there was the young woman I met in Baltimore who visited my home. It turned out that my impression of God's plans for her was accurate. The woman's name was Oprah Winfrey, and over the years she has indeed connected with and helped millions through her various business enterprises and philanthropy.

I have been one of those beneficiaries. While she was still in Baltimore, Oprah called to say she was doing a show on gospel music and wanted me to appear as her favorite male artist. Her invitation honored me because she believed in my gifts. That kind of contribution is priceless. Then, after Oprah left Baltimore to begin *The Oprah Winfrey Show* in Chicago, she encouraged the station to give me a one-hour slot to do a live weekly talk show. The two-and-a-half years I hosted *Sunday Live* proved to be an incredible training ground and opened doors for me to host other programs.

More recently, Oprah and her foundation have generously donated millions to the kids and programs of the US Dream Academy. One night at a fund-raising gala, she gave me the surprise of my life by handing me a check for one million dollars.

Do you see what can happen when you treat others with kindness? A little bit of compassion goes a very long way. The key is to think of others before yourself. Did Pat Pullen loan me five dollars because she expected to make a lifelong friend? Did I invite Oprah Winfrey to my home because I thought she would one day contribute to a cause I hadn't even imagined yet? Of course not. If you are kind because you are looking for a kickback, you will find yourself disappointed.

What you will discover, however, is that when you regularly practice the power of kindness, following Jesus' teaching by treating others the way you want to be treated, your focus moves away from yourself and onto others. You begin to see and meet the needs of those who are struggling. Strangely, you start to feel happier and more fulfilled. You begin to develop new relationships, some entirely unexpected. You may have less in terms of finances, at least for the time being, yet you somehow feel as if you have more. As time goes on, you notice that some of the blessings you've been giving out start coming back your way.

What has happened? You have begun to resemble, reflect, and reveal the character of God. You have moved a step closer to becoming the best *you* that you can be.

Your Kindness Quotient

In the Bible, Jesus makes it very clear that God values compassionate character. He tells the story of the Good Samaritan, a man who not only stopped to help an injured man at the side of the road but also transported him to an inn, spent the night there, and the next day paid the innkeeper to make sure the injured man would continue to receive care—all even though the hurt man, like most Jews at the time, viewed Samaritans with contempt.[10]

Likewise, Jesus tells us that when we feed the hungry, invite in a stranger, clothe those without covering, and visit someone in prison, it's as if we are doing the same for Him.[11] Our kindness toward the people around us—the pebbles that we drop in the water—ripple out until they touch God Himself. This is how we become more like Him.

To make godly kindness part of our everyday ethos, however, you and I need to consciously develop our compassion. The following are sixteen ideas that will help you enhance your kindness quotient:

1. Show mercy to others, remembering that God has done the same for you. Forgive them when they hurt you. "Kill" your enemies with kindness.
2. Demonstrate loyalty to others. Stick with them when times get rough. (Use common sense, however—not everyone deserves blind loyalty.)
3. Develop benevolence in your heart. Benevolence is undeserved kindness, and it enables you to be kind to those who are unkind to you.
4. Overflow with compassion. In response to other people's pain, make every effort to bring them comfort and solace. This includes people you may not know very well.
5. Express appreciation. Everyone needs to be noticed and recognized. Appreciation tells others that they have worth.
6. Cultivate gratitude. This is a little different from appreciation; in a way it needs to precede it. Be specifically thankful for both large and small aspects of your life. This will help you be content with your situation and will encourage you to share with others in need.

7. Show fairness to others. Another way of saying this is to be just, to act in a way that is free of prejudice and partiality.
8. Display generosity toward others. The giving of a gift, not the gift being given, is the greatest gift of all.
9. Express gentleness in touch and in speech. Gentleness—strength that is controlled by love—is vital to all aspects of kindness.
10. Engage others with sympathy. Allow yourself to be moved by someone's plight. Without sympathy, we are more like machines or animals than like God.
11. Grow in patience. Your patience shows that you value someone else enough to give up your time.
12. Look for deeper understanding. Put yourself in another person's shoes. An understanding person has matured past "me first."
13. Lower yourself in humility. Take your pride to the cleaners, and you will find it a lot easier to treat others with respect and kindness.
14. Defer to others as often as possible. Even if you do not agree with their decisions, you can acquiesce out of kindness. Even if they never learn from their mistakes, you can show them the kindness of humble deference.
15. "Infect" others with your cheerfulness. A kind person is peaceful and cheerful, which benefits everyone. Cheerfulness is contagious. Go out of your way to be positive.
16. Abide in peaceful trust. Trust in God's loving control of the circumstances of life. It is difficult to be kind when you are not peaceful (and it is difficult to be peaceful when you are not kind!).

A kind gesture is one of the most simple and profound actions that we can perform. When kindness becomes a habit, so ingrained within us that it is part of our character, it changes lives.

A couple named George and Mary Lou were celebrating their golden wedding anniversary. A reporter, noting that so many marriages end in divorce, wondered what secret had enabled them to keep their relationship strong for fifty years. "What is your recipe," the reporter asked George, "for a long, happy marriage?"

George answered that just after his wedding, his new father-in-law pulled him aside and gave him a gift. It was a gold wristwatch, one George still wore all these years later. He drew up his sleeve to show the reporter. Imprinted on the face of the watch were the words George had read and put into practice several times each day for the past five decades: "Say something nice to Mary Lou."[12]

So simple, yet so profound. I believe George is one man who discovered this aspect of God's best life for us.

Cultivating Kindness

Practicing kindness (or unkindness) has little impact on the inanimate objects that surround us. You can compliment your coffeemaker in the morning, but it won't feel any better or warm up any faster. You can yell insults at your computer, car, or phone and they won't react at all. Nothing will change.

But for flesh-and-blood people—our spouses, our children, our coworkers, the stranger in the store, the homeless man or woman on the street—a simple nod or gentle word can make all the difference. It did for the armed intruder at the backyard dinner party in Washington, DC. It did for the injured man helped by the Good Samaritan. It did for me, too, many times over.

To fully understand the power of kindness, we must also realize what happens to us when we generate it. No matter how much we appreciate the kindness of others, our lives will be so much richer, happier, and fuller if we make it a habit to *give* kindness as well as receive it. This is character that provides purpose for our existence. This is behavior that enables us to adopt the ethos of God.

Emily Dickinson captured this idea in one of her poems:

If I can stop one heart from breaking,
I shall not live in vain;
If I can ease one life the aching,
Or cool one pain,
Or help one fainting robin
Unto his nest again,
I shall not live in vain.[13]

All it takes is for you to take that first compassionate step. A little kindness can indeed go a very long way.

PRACTICING KINDNESS

We take a risk when we practice kindness. It pushes us out of our comfort zone. We don't know where it will lead or what it will cost. Yet the benefits so far outweigh the risks that there really is no other logical choice. If we want to live fulfilled, if we want to connect with our brothers and sisters, if we want to know and be more like God, and if we want to know God's best life for us, we must cultivate kindness.

As you review the following prerequisites for and by-products of kindness, consider which ones are already part of your ethos and which may need to be developed further.

Benevolence—When you are kind to someone who doesn't necessarily deserve it, you are showing benevolence. It means to rain copious showers of goodwill upon another person regardless of that person's attitude toward you.

Cheerfulness—A powerful shield of defense against worry, self-pity, and myriad forms of negativity, cheerfulness is one of the greatest allies of kindness.

Compassion—We reveal our compassion when we are moved to bring comfort and solace to those who are almost overwhelmed by anguish or agony.

Fairness—To be just is to be fair, to treat people impartially and with equanimity. It's easier to be kind when we remember that everyone is a child of God and deserves fair treatment.

Generosity—Kindness springs from a generous spirit. Amazingly, the act of being generous benefits the giver as much or more than the person who receives it.

Gentleness—When a powerful hand's first instinct is a soft touch, this is called gentleness. It is restraint combined with a desire for the good of another.

Gratitude—The more we adopt an attitude of gratitude, the easier it is to put our own problems aside and show kindness to the people around us.

Respect—The greatest form of respect is honoring those who will never be able to do anything for you. If you respect people only because they were created and are loved by God, kindness will follow.

Sympathy—When you are sympathetic, you are so moved by others' hardship and difficulties that you rally to their aid. It is one of the greatest traits of humanity.

Want to investigate kindness further? Return to our website at www.YourBestDestinyAssessment.com and take the assessment if you haven't already done so. On page 245 of this book, you can review the questions from the assessment that measure kindness.

BECOMING YOUR BEST YOU

How does God show kindness toward you?

Describe a situation from your own life in which merciful kindness was more effective than threats or punishment.

What aspect of kindness do you find most challenging?

After reading this chapter, what do you realize about the importance of kindness in your life?

Dear God, I expect to grow in kindness as I treat others with kindness, the way I myself would like to be treated. I need You to help me over the rough places, when my selfishness overcomes me. Give me more of Your character so that I can reflect it to others. Amen.

10

THE SPLENDOR OF LOVE

How to Experience the Deepest Love of All

What if he looks for someone else? The thought echoed through Beth's mind as she stared at herself in the dressing-room mirror. She had put on a few pounds in the twenty-two years they'd been married, and her hair was starting to gray. Maybe more importantly, she'd lost the easy smile she used to have, the sparkle in her eyes that showed she was ready for anything. What was she ready for now? She wasn't even sure. There was no denying it: She looked and felt middle-aged. She couldn't keep the niggling doubt away: *What if he looks for someone else?*

It seemed as if there was always something to prove, something she had to do to hold on to love before it slipped through her fingers. Be smarter. Accomplish more. Be prettier. Get in better shape. Be a better conversationalist. Get a promotion. The truth was, she was exhausted from keeping score in her relationships, tired of making sure she had more in the credit column than the debit. Sometimes she let herself imagine what it would be like to be loved for no reason at all, loved just because she was Beth. She imagined being so secure in a love that wouldn't fade that she would have more love to give, that she'd reach out to others from a sense of fullness instead of need. Now that would be a love worth having.

. . .

If we love each other, God lives in us, and
his love is brought to full expression in us.

1 JOHN 4:12

You could say that I met my future wife on a trip around the world.

The occasion was an event put on by the faculty at Oakwood College when I was a sophomore there. The professors opened up their homes to students, each providing food and entertainment from a different country. My classmates and I were to get on buses labeled with signs such as "Italian," "Spanish," or "West Indian." Once aboard, we would soon be transported to a local residence transformed into an exotic location.

My focus at the time was less on broadening my international education, however, and more on how I might meet a young woman I'd noticed my first week on campus that year. Her name was Linda Galloway. She looked like a dream and had what I call a "Jesus glow" about her.

When the time came for us to choose our countries, I spotted Linda and a friend stepping onto the bus headed for "Mexico." I quickly boarded the same bus and sat discreetly behind them. Soon, however, I heard Linda's friend say, "You know, I'm not really in the mood for tortillas and beans tonight. Why don't we try Chinese?" Before I knew it, Linda and her friend were hurrying off the bus and onto a new one. I followed a few paces behind, trying to be as inconspicuous as possible.

Chinese food must have been popular among Oakwood students, because this bus was packed. After Linda and her friend sat down, I squeezed into a seat in the back. To my dismay, however, Linda and her friend got up a minute later and again slipped off the bus. Had they noticed I was following them and decided to give me the brush-off? I had to find out, so I got up and shadowed them once more.

This time, the two young women boarded the "Soul Food"

bus. I settled into a seat right behind them. Meeting Linda was proving to be more difficult than I'd anticipated. I already felt as if I'd chased her around the world, and we hadn't even left the campus yet!

Afraid that Linda and her friend might change their minds once again, I waited until the bus started moving before I unleashed my less-than-original opening line: "What are two nice young women like you doing out alone on a night like this?"

Linda smiled and looked back at me with a charming blend of friendliness and reserve. "We're not alone," she said. "It looks as if you're the one who's alone." Her soft voice captivated me.

That evening marked the beginning of our relationship. Our first real date was a college-sponsored evening at a local roller-skating rink. I'd never been on roller skates before, so I told Linda that she would have to teach me. What a delightful experience to have the most beautiful young woman in the world solicitously holding my hand, even putting a steadying arm around my waist to help me get my balance as we practiced in Beginner's Alley. That night, I was in no great hurry to become a proficient skater.

We hadn't dated long when I realized that I was in love with Linda. We dedicated our relationship to the Lord and a few months later were engaged. It was only then that Linda revealed God had spoken to her shortly after we met, telling her, "That's the man you're going to marry."

Our wedding took place on a warm August day in Linda's hometown of Fort Pierce, Florida. I couldn't have been happier. I had been blessed by God with the chance to build what I had never had as a child: a happy home. And I would share it with the love of my life.

Love. We all know it's terribly important. We yearn for it, talk about it, write about it, dream about it. We sing about it in songs such as "Love Will Keep Us Together" and "All You Need Is Love." But what is love, really? And what does it have to do with living our God-given destiny?

Love has been explained as a strong emotion and as a virtue that encompasses human kindness, compassion, and affection. In the past, I have described love as choosing to be at your best when someone else is not at his or her best. We call it love when what we want is never most important and what the other person needs is always more important. Those simple four letters can express anything from our feelings about the mundane ("I love lasagna") to our deepest feelings for another ("I love you").

In perhaps its most profound definition, however, love can be described as the culmination of our efforts to resemble, reflect, and reveal the ethos of God. Each of the seven character qualities that we have already explored in this book—belief, virtue, wisdom, self-control, perseverance, sacredness, and kindness—leads to the next. When you and I develop our character in these areas, it's as if we are scaling a ladder. On the topmost rung of the ladder, we find love.

You may know the biblical story of Jacob, grandson of Abraham, the father of Israel. Jacob once had a dream in which he saw a ladder stretching from the earth all the way to heaven. God Himself stood at the top of the ladder.[1] Many Bible scholars have interpreted the ladder in Jacob's dream as representing God reaching out to His children through His Son, Jesus. He has already bridged the gap between Himself and us. But we can also think of the ladder as exemplifying a journey toward deepening our character and reflecting God's. When we climb the ladder—that is, when we make each of these character elements part of our ethos—we step closer to becoming like God, one rung at a time.

Much as we might want to, we can't jump straight to the top of the ladder. Our character development must incorporate all of the rungs, with each new step building upon what we've already cultivated. Many have tried, usually without even realizing it, to skip a few of the steps we've described. The result is that sooner or later, they lose their footing on the ladder and find themselves facedown in the dirt. They glimpse God's best life for them but never quite reach it. Maybe you know the feeling?

When we persist in growing deeper and stronger in each of the first seven elements of God's ethos, we at last begin to understand and embody the greatest of them all: love. Nothing is more holy. Nothing better reveals the essence of God's character. As the Bible tells us, God *is* love.[2] He showed love when He created the universe; when He revealed Himself to His people; when He sent His Son, Jesus; and when He sent the Holy Spirit as a guide and comforter. His love for His creation is beyond measure.

Love also represents the nuts and bolts that hold together all the other rungs in the ladder of godly character. We can't reach the top without it.

What does it look like to put all eight dimensions of character together? It is a rare sight. Most of us are still trying to identify where we need to grow so we can scale the ladder. But I know at least one person who is a truly amazing example of godly character. She has traveled a long journey, overcoming considerable obstacles to become a loving wife, a wonderful mother, a successful nurse, and a woman who's enjoyed unexpected opportunities to travel the world and dine with presidents. Far better than most, she understands what God's best life for us is all about.

Let me tell you more about my wife, Linda.

A Journey to Godly Character

Linda Galloway is the sixth of nine children. Her grandfather had been a slave in the South in the 1850s. Her father had married and raised a family. When his marriage dissolved, he married again, this time to a schoolmate of his son, a young woman one-third his age—Linda's mother.

Linda grew up in Fort Pierce, Florida, in a little green house with white awnings at 1707 North 13th Street. To say her childhood was tumultuous would be an understatement. Linda's father moved out when she was eight years old, leaving her young mother to raise the eight children still at home. Her mother had her hands full. Alcohol, drugs, guns, and arguments were common sights at home. Linda often had to resort to calling the police to keep the peace.

But Linda found a lifeline amidst the turmoil. It began when she was just three years old and a neighbor, a woman everyone called Sister Forbes, offered to have Linda spend weekends at her house. Linda's grateful mother accepted the offer.

Linda began attending church with the Forbes family. At first she didn't understand everything she was learning and wasn't dedicated to going. One day when she was eight, she told Sister Forbes she couldn't go to church because she was sick and didn't have clean socks. Sister Forbes knew Linda wasn't telling the truth, however. A few days later, Sister Forbes took Linda to some of the nicest stores in the town of Palm Beach. Linda tried on one beautiful dress after another, as well as all the accessories. Several ended up in the Forbes family car for the drive home.

On that drive, Linda dreamed of all those lovely clothes hanging in her closet, but it never happened. Sister Forbes kept the new clothes at her house. To wear them, she said, Linda had to come over and go to church with the Forbes family. (Today, I call that "Holy Ghost bribery"!)

Whatever the method, Linda was inspired to start attending church regularly. She quickly began to cherish her time there. Something about what she was learning and feeling made sense in her mind and her heart. At the age of twelve, she realized that she loved Jesus. She dedicated her life to Him. Without realizing it, Linda had embarked on a journey of developing the eight pillars of godly character.

Her faith took root and matured, sustaining her through continual conflicts at home. Linda felt that she could hear God's voice, and she sensed that an angel walked with her, guiding and protecting her steps. Her strong faith prepared her to climb higher on the ladder that stretched toward godly character.

The Galloway family had a long history of births out of wedlock. That history continued with Linda's brothers and sisters—all but one gave birth or fathered a child while unmarried. After her father left, Linda realized she didn't want to live in or someday raise her own children in a broken home. She said no to the dances and wild parties, as well as to premarital sex, alcohol, and drugs. With the help of her faith, Linda committed herself to the next rung in the ladder of godly character: a life of virtue.

The experience of combining belief and moral living showed Linda the wisdom of God's instruction. She was able to see what the rest of her family didn't understand—that there was a grand destiny waiting for each of them, one they could grasp if they only made better choices.

The combination of faith, virtue, and wisdom moved Linda farther up the ladder of godly character, enabling her to display exceptional self-control. Her restraint showed on the evening she was in her bedroom and checked her wallet, discovering that the money she'd set aside to give to the church that weekend was gone.

Linda was sure her brother had taken it, but she didn't start screaming about how she'd been robbed or accuse her brother of being a thief. Instead, she picked up her Bible and calmly walked into the living room where several members of the family were drinking and smoking. "Mama," she said, "I want whoever took my money to know that the Bible asks, 'Will a man rob God?' The answer is 'Oh yes, he will,' because somebody robbed God when he took the money I was going to give to the church out of my purse." She stared at her brother as she said it.

Linda's family often disparaged her faith in God, and this night was no exception. Everyone in the room laughed at her. "Oh, this child is too much," one sibling said. Yet by the next morning, the money was back in Linda's purse. By keeping her composure, she'd successfully resolved the problem—and perhaps given at least one member of the family something to think about.

You had to be tough if you were a Galloway who esteemed God as more important than anything. Linda's siblings challenged her again and again, sometimes verbally, other times by walking in dirty feet across a floor she'd just mopped. Despite the taunting and harassment, however, Linda didn't give in. She did not stray from the new path she'd chosen. She persevered. Linda is the most determined person I've ever known, possessing what Sister Forbes called "stickability." When she was a teen, she told her mother, "I know they say the apple doesn't fall far from the tree. But this is one apple that's going to keep rolling and rolling and rolling."

Linda stepped even higher on the ladder of godly character when she developed a strong sense of the sacred. To keep the

Sabbath holy, she completed all her chores before sunset on Friday. When Linda was twelve, she attended a Bible study at her church. One of her mentors, Sister Buckley, encouraged her and her class by saying, "You are never too young to ask God for what you want in life and you are never too young to ask for a good Christian husband." That sounded like a fine idea to Linda. She wanted a husband, a home, and a family that honored everything holy. She began asking God for these things.

The next step on the ladder of godly character is kindness. I believe that my wife is naturally kind, but her experiences while growing up and her unwavering commitment to God and to developing her character increased her compassion a hundredfold. She saw it modeled by the care and attentions over the years of Sister Forbes, who gave Linda a safe haven every weekend, nourished her spiritual side, and lifted her self-esteem, frequently reminding her that she was a "pretty girl." It was Brenda Joyce, however, who brought out the full measure of Linda's kindness.

Brenda Joyce was Linda's sister, five years older. She'd been dropped as a baby, leading to what was probably cerebral palsy. Brenda Joyce was smart, but she couldn't talk and her growth was stunted. She lived at home and slept in Linda's room—throughout Linda's teen years, she took care of her sister, making sure she was fed, dressed, and comfortable. Linda also sang and read Scripture to Brenda Joyce. Linda's amazing, daily compassion gave her sister a sense of value and hope for the next day. It also moved Linda even higher on the ladder of godly character.

Belief. Virtue. Wisdom. Self-control. Perseverance. Sacredness. Kindness. When you fully develop your character in these seven areas, you almost can't help fulfilling the final and most exalted dimension of character: love. It is the vital ingredient that enables us to most fully reflect the glory of Christ. Without it, we will never truly bless those around us or realize our best destiny. With it, we have the means to know joy, peace, and fulfillment—and to change the world.

As the Bible says so eloquently:

> If I could speak all the languages of earth and of angels, but didn't love others, I would only be a noisy gong or a clanging cymbal. If I had the gift of prophecy, and if I understood all of God's secret plans and possessed all knowledge, and if I had such faith that I could move mountains, but didn't love others, I would be nothing. If I gave everything I have to the poor and even sacrificed my body, I could boast about it; but if I didn't love others, I would have gained nothing.
>
> Love is patient and kind. Love is not jealous or boastful or proud or rude. It does not demand its own way. It is not irritable, and it keeps no record of being wronged. It does not rejoice about injustice but rejoices whenever the truth wins out. Love never gives up, never loses faith, is always hopeful, and endures through every circumstance. . . .
>
> Three things will last forever—faith, hope, and love—and the greatest of these is love.[3]

It was love that kept Linda rooted in her place when her mother's angry boyfriend pulled out a gun and waved it at her family. The rest of them could run away, but Brenda Joyce was also there, and she couldn't move. So Linda, her heart pounding, stood her ground. With the boyfriend watching, Linda picked up the phone and called the police, asking them to come defuse the situation.

It was also love that inspired Linda to care for others by pursuing a career in nursing, first in Nashville and then at Oakwood in Alabama. And it was love again that has made her such an incredible wife to me and an amazing mother to our three sons.

A life without love is a life that lacks meaning. We *need* to love and be loved. Yet there is more than one kind of love. If we are to fully understand it and make it part of our character, we must explore the facets of love in more detail.

The Beauty of Romantic Love

We can divide love into three types—romantic love, which the ancient Greeks called *eros*; brotherly love, or *philia*; and unconditional, sacrificial love, known as *agape*.

Almost everyone has experienced romantic love. It is instinctual, part of our inner biology. Without it, men and women would not pair up, have children, and form families. Romantic love is characterized by beauty, purity, and creativity.

Do you remember the warmth and glow of your first romantic love? A flame of attachment began to burn brightly in your soul, filling you with admiration and desire. You could say this kind of love is like a powerful booster rocket that puts you into orbit around another person. Yet as a booster rocket is used up and falls away after it propels its payload into space, the fire and excitement of romantic love also often falls away. Because so many couples are tied to the feelings of love, especially the spontaneity of new love, they go their separate ways without experiencing the profound aspects of love that come with faithfulness, commitment, and time. You know what I'm talking about: the intimacy of a secret, a shared glance. Holding hands when no words are needed.

Hearing and supporting the deepest desires of each other's hearts. Spending time together and doing things for each other—just because.

Such relationships can be fragile, however. Too often, we are tempted to take those we love for granted. This is why it is so important to commit to honoring one another and staying faithful to each other. Only when we keep the purity of our love intact are we blessed to experience the joy and completeness it brings.

Linda and I still share the joy of romantic love. But I meet so many husbands and wives who do not. They have become little more than roommates. Affairs intended to quell the boredom instead push them farther apart. So many of those marriages end in divorce, and even those that survive are often hollow and loveless. It doesn't have to be that way. Life doesn't have to suck the love and passion out of marriage. To keep the flame of romantic love burning, though, you must make it a priority in your life. You must also cherish everything good about your partner and forgive the flaws.

On February 11, 1990, on a warm summer day, I was privileged to be a silent witness to history. I stood with the crowd in front of Cape Town City Hall to welcome Nelson Mandela as he walked out of prison after more than twenty-seven years in captivity. After he was elected president of South Africa, Mandela became known for his wisdom as he worked to unite a nation divided by apartheid. But Mandela also spoke out on other subjects, including love. He once said, "When you love a woman, you don't see her faults. The love is everything. You don't pay attention to the things others may find wrong with her. You just love her."[4]

Romantic love is wonderful when you nourish it and allow it to grow. Value yourself and your loved one. Practice the character traits of discipline, respect, and self-control. All things of value must be protected and tended. After all, you would not leave a beautiful diamond lying around where it could be lost or stolen. You take good care of your home and your car. You guard your health by disciplining yourself to eat well and exercise. When you find yourself in a romantic relationship, guard what you've found.

In a similar way, we must also guard our relationship with God. When we take Him for granted and grow distant from Him, our character begins to deteriorate and our lives suffer. Romantic love can be a model of what our relationship with God should look like: pure, faithful, close, and unconditional.

Whether you've been together for a week, a decade, or a lifetime, treat the one you love with tenderness and respect. Only after we have faithfully pursued this course for years will we fully realize the gift of *eros*—a deep and lasting love that comforts us when times are hard, rejoices with us when times are good, and moves us into deeper intimacy with God.

The Nobility of Brotherly Love

The term the Greeks used for the kind of love you might feel for a close friend is *philia*. It is also called "brotherly love." It is a love so strong that you might feel the same about your friend as about a biological brother or sister.

Many remarkable friendships are recounted in literature. Anne Shirley and Diane Barry in L. M. Montgomery's delightful novel, *Anne of Green Gables*. Sherlock Holmes and Dr. Watson in Sir Arthur Conan Doyle's Sherlock Holmes series. Frodo Baggins and Samwise Gamgee in J. R. R. Tolkien's classic, *The Lord of the Rings*.

These relationships are fictional, but each paints a beautiful picture of what great friendship, true brotherly love, can be.

The Bible includes the story of an amazing friendship between two young men named Jonathan and David. Jonathan was a child of privilege: He was the oldest son of Saul, the reigning king of ancient Israel. David was the youngest son of a commoner. He took care of the sheep for his father.

When David's brothers went off to battle the Philistines, his father held him back because he was young and someone had to care for things at home. One day, however, David visited the battlefield and did the unthinkable. He stepped forward and answered the challenge of a giant Philistine, Goliath. Against all odds, David used a slingshot to knock the giant out. David cut off Goliath's head with the giant's own sword and delivered it to King Saul.

That was the day David met Jonathan, and the two young men became fast friends. Saul kept David on at the palace rather than sending him back to his shepherding duties. And before long, Jonathan made a special vow of friendship with David and sealed it by giving him his robe, tunic, sword, and belt.

Saul greatly favored David at first, but soon the king became jealous of David's popularity with the people. Saul became obsessed with assassinating David. Although he promised Jonathan that no harm would come to David, he later made another attempt on David's life.

When Jonathan realized his father's duplicity, he was both angry at his father and fearful for his friend. He and David made a pact, affirming their friendship for each other as long as they both lived. David also promised to show faithful love to Jonathan's family if Jonathan should die before him. Later, David learned that his friend Jonathan had been killed in battle alongside his father, King Saul. He was deeply grieved.

In due time, David became the king over all of Israel and assumed the many responsibilities of leading a nation. Yet David remembered his promise to his friend. He set out to learn whether anyone in Saul and Jonathan's family was still alive. Eventually, he discovered that one of Jonathan's sons, a helpless cripple named Mephibosheth, had survived. David sent for Mephibosheth and asked him to visit David at the palace. When the man arrived, David bestowed on him all the land that once had belonged to Saul and offered him a permanent home in the royal palace.[5] David showed the depth of his friendship for Jonathan, a love so strong and noble that it flourished even after Jonathan's death.

We still find examples of this kind of friendship today. Pro basketball greats Larry Bird and Magic Johnson developed a deep and lasting friendship that overcame race, rivalry, and the trauma of the news in 1991 that Magic had tested positive for HIV.

"The best feeling is when a friend supports you," Magic Johnson said recently. "And this young man came and supported me. Forget the sports, forget the championships, forget the MVP. He came to my side and supported me and I'll never forget that."[6]

What kind of friends do you have? Are they just acquaintances? Does their friendship come and go with your popularity or lack of it? If so, they are false friends. They do not offer *philia* love. And how do you regard them? Are you there for them when they need you? Do you demonstrate honesty and faithfulness no matter the circumstances?

Being there for your friends, telling them the truth when their actions are hurtful or self-serving, drawing out the best in them—this is what develops godly character and shows *philia* love.

The Greatest Love of All

One type of love both transcends the others and is reflected in them. It is the kind of love that comes from God and resonates within us. The Greeks called it *agape.* When we love with *agape,* we reflect the character of God at the highest level.

Probably the most defining aspect of *agape* love is that it is unnatural. We cannot create it within ourselves, but we can receive it from God and pass it on to others. Have you experienced this type of love?

It works like this. God loved us first by His own choice and design, and He backed up that love with His actions, giving us redemption, forgiveness, and salvation. He waits for us to love Him back by our own choice and design. When we do, the connection is complete and the love of God flows into us. Yes, it is very much a miracle!

As much as I love Linda, loving God is my life's greatest romance. When I bow my head to pray, I feel something like what a blind woman must feel like while waiting for the arrival of her lover. I can't see His face, but I can sense His presence and hear His voice. And when I receive God's love, I can't help but show it in my interactions with others. It flows freely out of me to people I could never love otherwise. It makes me a better person, a godlier person.

Though we have chosen to speak of *agape* at the end of this book, it is not only the result of good character but also the source of it. In one sense, the other pillars lead us into it, since it's impossible to have true *agape* love without faith in the God who is the source of that love or without the self-control to act on it. But in another sense, *agape* empowers all the other aspects of love and godly character. It brings them to life and deepens them.

Your natural self might find it difficult to be honest at all times. Yet God's love—that perfect, sacrificial love flowing into you—gives you the power to achieve exactly that. You might find it difficult to perform a task with excellence. But when that task is done out of love for God, there is no thought of doing less than your best.

You might find it difficult to do the right thing, to speak love to the unlovely, to give of yourself unselfishly, to act with kindness, to rightly discern the needs of others, or to be wise and understanding. When you find it difficult to exhibit good character in any area of your life, *agape* love is the key to overcoming. It both regulates your contrary passions and transforms your character. The Bible tells us, "Dear friends, since God loved us that much, we surely ought to love each other. No one has ever seen God. But if we love each other, God lives in us, and his love is brought to full expression in us."[7]

This love God has for us, this love that He asks us to pass along to others, is wider than our imaginations, softer than our most tender thoughts, deeper than our greatest affection, stronger than a lion's heart. God's love perseveres in its gentle purposes toward us, winning our devotion and surrounding us with tokens of His compassionate care.

Love has become the cornerstone of my faith. It triumphs over my doubts and bitterness and conquers all my anxiety and fears. Won't you give God your heart? It's the only way to become the person you were created to be.

God's love is inviting rather than coercing. He has given you full control over how you will live your life. He will not interfere.

He wants you to love Him fully and freely. Won't you reach out to Him and receive His love? Won't you accept His challenge to become the best you that you can be, putting together all these core dimensions of His character? Won't you ask Him to help you fulfill your supreme destiny? That, after all, is God's best life for you.

The choice is yours.

Learning to Love

Love can be described in a thousand ways and comes in a thousand forms. Of all those forms, however, none means more to us than one that involves the ultimate sacrifice. Charlie Coker, a World War II veteran, understands this personally.

Coker and his buddy Julian Shamrose were among the US soldiers fighting on the Pacific island of Okinawa in the spring of 1945. Coker was a machine gunner, but during a break in the action, he left his post to help repair an axle on an amphibious tractor. When bullets from enemy aircraft suddenly began to rain down on them, Shamrose jumped behind Coker's .50-caliber gun to return fire.

Shamrose was killed in the attack.

"I fell down on the ground and cried to the Lord," Coker said years later. "He died for me, took my place."[8]

More than two thousand years ago, Jesus did the same thing on a wooden cross. He died for you and me, taking the punishment that should have been ours. It was the ultimate sacrifice, the perfect model for you and me, and the final secret to acquiring godly character.

It was love at its fullest and finest.

DEVELOPING LOVING CHARACTER

Love can be a difficult concept to pin down. It encompasses a wide spectrum of actions, attitudes, and emotions—yet we certainly know it when we feel it or when we're in it. And we nearly always welcome it.

So does God. He is both the author of love and the perfect embodiment of it. It is when we learn to love—fully, unselfishly, unreservedly—that we most closely resemble His character and ethos.

The list below includes only a few of the many prerequisites for and by-products of a loving character. As you ponder each, consider which are already established as part of your ethos and which you would like to add.

Affection—Sometimes when we least expect it, we can be overwhelmed by tender, warm feelings toward another. A show of affection can melt the coldest heart.

Attentiveness—An attentive person is especially observant, always mindful of and ready to assist with the needs and comfort of others.

Availability—Do you make yourself available when someone you love has a need? Availability has everything to do with being focused on others rather than self.

Commitment—One of the most loving acts of all is commitment. It is based not on temporary feelings but on a decision that lasts a lifetime.

Dependability—We show our love for others when we become someone they can trust and rely on. When we say we will do something, there is no question that we will do it.

Encouragement—A person who inspires with courage, spirit, or hope is an encourager. He or she has the ability to lift others no matter how bleak their circumstances.

Ingenuity—You can turn up the heat on romantic love by bringing a creative and clever spirit to your relationship.

Security—For many, nothing shows love like a spouse who provides a secure environment at home. That can mean working hard to support a family financially or being supportive and nonjudgmental during conversations.

Sensitivity—A sensitive person displays a special awareness of the attitudes and feelings of the people around him or her.

As is the case for each of the eight core dimensions of character listed in this book, you can learn more about additional characteristics of love by visiting our website at www.YourBestDestinyAssessment.com. See page 249 of this book to read the questions on the assessment that measure love.

BECOMING YOUR BEST YOU

In what ways has God demonstrated love to you personally?

How has love, either given or received, changed your life?

In what ways do you struggle to give or receive love?

In what tangible ways can love change the world?

Dear God, help me to see and understand that nothing can stand in the way of Your love. Show me how to make love both the foundation and pinnacle of my character. Please use me to love and change the world. Amen.

11

A PRESCRIPTION FOR TRANSFORMATION

How to Find Lasting Change

The great thing in this world is not so much where we stand as in what direction we are moving.

OLIVER WENDELL HOLMES

IN THIS BOOK, we've named and explored eight vital dimensions of character that can enable you to resemble, reflect, and reveal the ethos of God. What will you do with all this information? You have the tools to identify where you stand and where you want to be. But information without transformation results in stagnation. The challenge now is to make the change—to turn your weaknesses in the areas of belief, virtue, wisdom, self-control, perseverance, sacredness, kindness, and love into strengths so that you can discover your amazing destiny.

I want to give you a prescription for transformation. Dramatic personal change does not come naturally or easily to any of us. It usually requires hard work and sacrifice on our part. This is why you must discover what will give you that extra motivation to succeed. Your driving force must be exponentially more important to you than the costs of transformation.

For US Olympian Edwin Moses, that driving force was the thrill of competition. He loved testing himself against others and against his own standards. He also loved winning. Moses dominated the 400-meter hurdles like no one before or since, triumphing in every race he ran for nearly a decade and capturing Olympic gold medals in 1976 and 1984. His sacrifices were many—long hours of disciplined training, a restrictive diet, a limited social life. But for Moses, the rewards of victory on the track far outweighed the costs.

What, then, will drive you to transform your character weaknesses into strengths? It is different for every person. In my case, it is the favor of God. I am desperate to have His protection, provision, power, peace, and presence in my life. I can't live without them. And I know that my ultimate goal—to resemble, reflect, and reveal the character of God—will not be possible unless I have His favor.

How about you? What will motivate you to undergo character transformation? Will it be God's love? The desire to be the man or woman your family needs you to be? An unquenchable longing to know and be more like Christ? A yearning for fulfillment and purpose? Whatever the case may be, I encourage you to discover your driving force and embrace it. It is a key ingredient to a changed life.

It is not, however, the only ingredient. Motivation is essential, as is willpower, but by themselves they are not enough to achieve transformation. We must also join forces with the one who created us and our destiny. To turn weakness into strength, we must tap into the power of God.

Perhaps you feel a bit unworthy of God's help at this point. You have been reflecting on your character and have realized that in some areas you fall far short of the person you desire to be. Even the qualities you thought were your strengths need improvement. You may feel overwhelmed by your shortcomings of character and may think that God can't work with a person with so many flaws.

Let me assure you that this isn't the case! God has a special place in His heart for the weak, the meek, and the humble. In fact, it is through our weakness that He seems to do His best work. The apostle Paul said as much:

> So to keep me from becoming proud, I was given a thorn in my flesh, a messenger from Satan to torment me and keep me from becoming proud.
>
> Three different times I begged the Lord to take it away. Each time he said, "My grace is all you need. My power works best in weakness." So now I am glad to boast about my weaknesses, so that the power of Christ can work through me. That's why I take pleasure in my weaknesses, and in the insults, hardships, persecutions, and troubles that I suffer for Christ. For when I am weak, then I am strong.[1]

The "thorn" in Paul's side was likely a physical problem rather than a character defect, but the concept is the same. In this passage, God was telling Paul—and us—that, when we rely completely on His grace, we gain His power. You and I don't need to be discouraged about undeveloped character. We can be heartened by it because our limitations drive us toward the God who loves us and wants to transform us: "For when I am weak, then I am strong."

A man named Jordan discovered this several years ago. Jordan showed up at a Christian conference with a cold and weary heart. At the beginning of the conference, he had trouble joining with others to sing praise songs to God. Often he didn't even try. When a conference speaker invited people to confess and repent of their sins, however, something happened to Jordan. As he watched men and women leave their bleacher seats, walk to the front of the gymnasium, and publicly reveal their struggles, Jordan realized that he needed to do the same. That night, he wrote a four-page letter of confession to God.

The next day, Jordan read the letter aloud to the conference attendees. With his wife standing by his side, he admitted to a long list of failings, including impure motives; a desire for recognition; caring more about projects and tasks than people; a critical and judgmental spirit; keeping people at arm's length; a spirit of jealousy and envy; and addictions to overeating, spending, and pornography. For a long time, Jordan's character had been collapsing.

Jordan also read aloud, "I want these things to change. I want repentance. I want brokenness. Please pray that in the months ahead God will place within me a deep brokenness and create within me a new, clean heart—a heart that loves Him more than my own life."[2] Jordan had found his motivation to begin the process of transformation.

When he was done reading his letter, Jordan was surrounded by compassionate men and women who prayed for him, hugged and forgave him, and expressed their love for him. His confession, combined with this encouraging response, gave him a sense of release and joy. He felt he'd taken a tangible step toward the Lord. Later that evening, he joined in with others in some of the same worship songs that had opened the conference. This time, Jordan sang with enthusiasm, tears streaming down his cheeks.

The change in Jordan was more than fleeting. Over the next few years, he found that his weaknesses could indeed be turned into strengths. His character changed in ways he hadn't thought possible—all because he chose to rely on God. His wife wrote about it to a friend:

> Jordan continues to keep his relationship with God fresh and open. He has a goal to read the Bible this year, and for two years we have faithfully prayed together nightly before we go to sleep. He has kept his commitment to me, to himself, and to the Lord—not flawlessly, but it's our humanness that reminds us both of our never-ending, always present need for the Savior.[3]

Jordan's victory can also be yours. The character weaknesses that are holding you back can become the triggers that usher you into the ethos of God. As we can see from Jordan's example, this radical transformation begins with identifying the personal motivation that will inspire change. It also depends on connecting to the power that can be found only in God.

From Weakness to Strength

The process of moving from character weakness to character strength is more than an abstract or theoretical exercise. It involves mind, body, and spirit, and it requires intentional and concrete acts on our part. Remember that Jordan did more than simply identify his weaknesses. He also publicly confessed them and took specific steps to invite God to change them.

Let's explore practical ways to transform your character defects into areas of strength. I recommend the following six-step plan.

1. Assess Your Character and Examine Yourself

This book has already provided a useful foundation for evaluating your godly character. You now have the opportunity to take advantage of every pillar. Read and reread the previous chapters. Answer the discussion questions. Write down the prerequisites and by-products of each character dimension that you already possess and that you still hope to acquire and develop. Check out our website at www.YourBestDestinyAssessment.com to find out more about the quality of your character in each vital area.

The practice of assessing ourselves is both time honored and holy. When the early Christians gathered to remember Christ and partake in Communion, they were encouraged to appraise their motives before joining in: "That is why you should examine yourself before eating the bread and drinking the cup. For if you eat the bread or drink the cup without honoring the body of Christ, you are eating and drinking God's judgment upon yourself."[4]

In a similar way, we should examine ourselves before seeking to change our character through God's power. When we take the time to honestly evaluate where we stand, we are left with a much clearer understanding of our strengths and weaknesses and where we need to go next.

2. Acknowledge Your Weaknesses

We were not created to carry our burdens through this world alone. Our families and our friends are allies in our quest to transform our character. But they are unlikely to help us if we don't tell them what we're struggling with. It is human nature to pretend that we have it all together, to cover up our problems and flaws. Drawing back the curtain on our defects makes us feel exposed and weak. Yet this is precisely what we must do if we hope to turn our weakness into strength.

I'm not saying that we need to broadcast our troubles to the world. Yet when we open up about our imperfections to individuals we trust, we enlist new resources that can encourage us and lead us into our best destiny. The irony is that the more we reveal weakness, the greater our potential to move into a position of power. As modern philosopher Criss Jami has said, "To share your weakness is to make yourself vulnerable; to make yourself vulnerable is to show your strength."[5]

Of course, the greatest vulnerability is to acknowledge our weaknesses to God. For me, there is something special about the psalms composed by David—perhaps because he is a fellow musician. In his intimate conversations with God, I find a naked honesty that shows me where I'm falling short even as it encourages me. In one of those psalms, we glimpse the power of confession. David apparently did not admit to an unspecified offense and suffered for it. When he at last came clean with God, his physical and emotional troubles faded and he found new strength.

> When I refused to confess my sin,
>   my body wasted away,
>   and I groaned all day long.
> Day and night your hand of discipline was heavy on me.
>   My strength evaporated like water in the summer heat.

Finally, I confessed all my sins to you
and stopped trying to hide my guilt.
I said to myself, "I will confess my rebellion to the LORD."
And you forgave me! All my guilt is gone.[6]

Admitting our weaknesses to God can be difficult, but it brings us freedom. When we confess our failings instead of trying to hide them, God forgives us and lets us start again. Yet we won't improve until we accept the truth of who we are right now. We're stuck in place if we make excuses for our character or pretend that it will get better by itself. Instead, we must take a clear-eyed view of any behavior that is not in harmony with the will and purpose of God. Then we accept that this needs to change—both for our good and so that God's purpose will be fulfilled in our life.

3. Ask God for Help

Throughout our history, we Americans have demonstrated an amazing self-sufficiency. That rugged individualism enabled us to declare our independence and form a proud new nation. Sometimes, however, we take our individualism to extremes. We try to be the Lone Ranger, solving every problem on our own. Today, too many of us miss out on our best destiny because we're so determined to take on troubles—and improve our character—with no assistance from anyone. Instead, we should reach out to God.

God makes it clear, after all, that He wants us to ask Him for help. The Bible tells us, "Do not be anxious about anything, but in every situation, by prayer and petition, with thanksgiving, present your requests to God."[7] Notice that this verse does not say, "Try to fix your problems on your own, and if that doesn't work, come to Me." We are to go to God with our requests in every situation.

Jesus also told us, "Apart from me you can do nothing."[8] It would seem that Christ does not expect us to accomplish great things on our own. He knows who holds the power. It follows that if we plan to take on the ethos of God—a plan He most heartily approves of—He will expect and even require that we do so not through personal willpower but through His participation.

Just as important as the act of asking, however, is the manner in which we ask. God is not a genie standing by to grant our every wish. If we truly hope to transform our character, we need to approach Him in humility. The Bible says that "the Lord is close to the brokenhearted; he rescues those whose spirits are crushed."[9] This is the attitude we need to adopt if we hope for His help—not one of a master calling on a servant but of a weak and broken being who is in need of rescue.

4. Alter Your Attitude

One way God helps us is by changing the way we think—our attitudes.

An attitude is a settled way of thinking or feeling about something. Our attitudes are formed over years and based on our experiences, and they're powerful. Even if these thought patterns are unconscious, they're reflected in the way we act. We see this in children all the time. A girl who believes that she's not athletic may not go after a loose ball in a soccer game because she assumes she won't be able to reach it first. A boy who perceives himself as unintelligent may not pay attention when the teacher presents a new concept because he's already sure he just won't get it. A child who frequently feels left out may not reach out to try to make a new friend. Our patterns of thinking affect our actions.

Before we can be transformed, we have to be willing to let go of our settled ways of thinking about ourselves, our habits, our behavior, and even our addictions and pleasures. We have to allow God to disrupt them. The Bible tells us, "Let God transform you into a new person by changing the way you think."[10] This kind of change can be upsetting because it challenges core assumptions that we've held for a long time. But even though it may be uncomfortable now, the result will be worth it.

We need to learn to love ourselves, recognizing that we are not hopeless or stuck in our patterns. With God's help, we can change!

What attitudes do you need to let go of? Do you think about yourself in negative ways, perhaps as someone who can never improve? Do you have certain patterns of thinking that are sabotaging you as you seek to reflect God's character? Ask Him to change your patterns of thinking.

5. Abide in the Presence of God

We know from Scripture that Jesus gave His disciples the image of a grapevine and its branches as a picture of His relationship to them. A branch separated from its life-giving vine will never produce fruit. This is why Jesus said to His followers, "If you remain in me and my words remain in you, ask whatever you wish, and it will be done for you."[11]

Our requests—including the crucial goal of adopting the character of God—will be granted only when we abide in His presence and learn to want what He wants. How do we do that? As with the ethos of God, it begins with belief.

Our God is an invisible reality. To experience and remain in

Him, we must fully open our minds and hearts to the possibility of His presence. It is not something we strive for when the mood strikes us. Rather, it is a continuing process, cultivated moment by moment for a lifetime.

When our belief is activated this way, we can sense the nearness of God. It's as if we're aware of the molecular makeup of a room changing the instant God enters, and then we experience peace and a sense of His favor. Living for that awareness of God's presence is the greatest reward we can know. The reality is that we cannot transform our character weaknesses into strengths without mastering this discipline: seeking and sensing the presence of God. Not only is it a deterrent to sinful thoughts and actions, but it can be our greatest source of joy.

Imagine that you're in a concert hall, listening to a symphony. Sometimes you hear quiet passages where just a few string instruments are playing with great poignancy, and sometimes you hear grand, bombastic passages that are so exciting they pin you to your seat. And then at times you hear interludes of silence.

Too often we see our lives as a symphony of activity punctuated by brief moments of silence and reflection. But to live a transformed life, we need to turn that on its head. We must see our lives as a symphony of communion with the presence of God, punctuated by the distractions of our daily lives. The symphony of a transformed life is a life caught up in this sweet sense of the presence of God.

How can we cultivate it? We have already seen the importance of prayer in maintaining a relationship with God. To abide in Him, we must maintain an honest and ongoing conversation.

God seeks more from us, however. He desires that we offer Him the praise, honor, and respect He is due: "Give to the Lord the glory he deserves! Bring your offering and come into his presence. Worship the LORD in all his holy splendor."[12] This isn't for His benefit but for ours. Whether it is in church or in conversation with others, regularly praising God reminds us of our source of love and power and keeps us close to Him.

If we expect to abide in God's presence, we must also study and become intimately acquainted with His Word. It is a window into His ethos and is our instruction book for life.

Perhaps just as important as any of these steps is taking time to simply "be" with our Creator: "Be still, and know that I am God!"[13] In our increasingly fast-paced society, it's easy to neglect the practice of sitting down without an agenda and allowing God to speak to us and fill us with His presence. This is the work of the Holy Spirit, and we cannot transform our character weaknesses into strengths without Him.

William Temple, a bishop in the Church of England, used the example of Shakespeare to explain:

> It is no good giving me a play like *Hamlet* or *King Lear*, and telling me to write a play just like it. Shakespeare could do it; I can't. And it is no good showing me a life like the life of Jesus and telling me to live a life like it. Jesus could do it; I can't. But if the genius of Shakespeare could come and live inside me, I would then be able to write plays like he did. And if the Spirit of Jesus could come and live inside me, I would then be able to live a life like he did.[14]

In chapter 8 I mentioned the life-changing experience of watching the evangelist Dr. Cleveland prepare to speak. After seeing his example, I developed my own "preflight checklist" that helps me enter into the presence of God before I speak or sing. But one day I had been fooling around before I got up to speak—no moral failure, but not going through my regular routine to help me focus on the Lord. As I put my foot on the first step of the podium, it seemed that I heard a voice speak from heaven, saying, "Excuse me, son. I'm sorry, but I'm not going up with you today. You're on your own."

I was left with no choice but to go before the people and fake it. I had the same rising and falling of the voice and the same gesticulation I always did—but this time it was hollow. God's glory had departed. I had no sense of His presence.

Afterward I got down on my knees and begged God not to let me go through that again. I never wanted to perform without the sweet, overwhelming sense of His presence. Because for me, there is no greater joy than experiencing God's presence and basking in His love and blessings. This is what drives me to align my character with His. The benefits and rewards so far outweigh any sacrifices I must make to adopt God's ethos that they can't be compared. If you choose to abide in His presence, I believe you will see what I mean.

6. Activate God's Power

A few simple and practical steps can help us activate God's power and complete the process of transforming our character. Let's take a look at each of them.

- *Adopt a positive mind-set.* Michael Jordan was a fifteen-year-old sophomore when he tried out for his high school basketball team, expecting to make the varsity. When the coach assigned him to the JV team instead, Jordan could have given up on his basketball ambitions right then. But he didn't. He used the perceived snub as motivation to get better. "My attitude is that if you push me towards something that you think is a weakness," Jordan said, "then I will turn that perceived weakness into a strength."[15]

Jordan had already made up his mind that he would be successful. What followed was one of the greatest careers in the history of basketball, which included five NBA Most Valuable Player awards and six world championships. It all began with Jordan's positive attitude.

The Bible tells of a man named Nehemiah who also exemplified a positive mind-set. In exile with many of his people, he heard that the walls and gates of Jerusalem had been destroyed. Distraught about the condition of his homeland, he asked the king for permission to return to Jerusalem and rebuild the walls that provided the city's protection. When the king not only agreed to Nehemiah's request but also provided some of his own resources as building materials and some of his soldiers as protection, Nehemiah was sure that God was behind the project. In fact, he was so sure that he did not allow himself to be discouraged even when he arrived and saw with his own eyes the huge task in front of him. Local officials scoffed at him, but Nehemiah was not shaken. He told them, "The God of heaven will help us succeed. We, his servants, will start rebuilding this wall."[16]

Nehemiah's positive mind-set gave him the motivation to come up with a plan and put it into practice. When enemies threatened to attack, Nehemiah simply divided his work force into two groups and had half of them work while the other half served as guards. He told his people, "Don't be afraid of the enemy! Remember the Lord, who is great and glorious."[17] His relentless positivity meant that Jerusalem's walls and gates were rebuilt in just fifty-two days[18]—a huge accomplishment in a time when all construction work was done by hand.

Nehemiah's success can be ours as well. When we are near to God and believe in our hearts that we can align with His desires for our life, we have access to the greatest power in the universe. Anything is possible: "For I can do everything through Christ, who gives me strength."[19] *All* of our character weaknesses can be turned into strengths when we allow those weaknesses to drive us closer to Him.

- *Adopt a vision.* It can be incredibly inspiring to have a picture of who and what you want to be. Most often, that vision comes courtesy of others. When I was fifteen and my voice changed, I loved to sing but had no vocal teacher. I heard an amazing voice singing on the radio during that time, and that voice became my instructor. I began to imitate this singer's style. I had found a vision of someone doing what I loved to do.

  Years later, I purchased tickets for my wife and me to watch this same man perform in Las Vegas. Something told me to also reach out to him. I e-mailed, letting him know that his inspiration had helped me realize everything I could have imagined in my music career. I got an e-mail back inviting Linda and me to visit him after the show. His eyes widened with surprise and delight when I walked in singing, "It's not unusual to be loved by anyone." Sir Tom Jones was my musical North Star.

Do you need to be wiser? Show greater self-control? Be more holy? Identify someone who will give you a vision of what that looks like and you'll find new inspiration to get there yourself.

- *Set realistic goals.* We are more likely to stay encouraged when we write down a series of reasonable goals. If kindness and compassion are challenges for you, don't immediately commit to a yearlong program to serve the poor. Instead, plan on performing at least one kind act a day for the next week. If you are successful, increase to two kind acts a day the next week. When you can see and measure your progress over the long term, you're more apt to remain in pursuit of your goals and allow God to do His work in you for a lifetime.
- *Use your strengths.* Our best qualities can be assets in helping us overcome our weaknesses. A coworker may be great at sharing ideas with others orally but may be a poor writer. So what does he do when he has an idea that can save his company thousands next year? He arranges to present his proposal in a meeting with company leadership, using computer images to support his talk.

  In a similar way, we can lean on our character strengths to offset or overcome our shortcomings. Maybe you know how to persevere but are low on wisdom. If you rely on that perseverance to work on increasing your wisdom quotient week after week, you're much more likely to succeed. Or perhaps you are overflowing with love for the people around you, but you struggle with self-control. Consider how developing your self-control will enable you to better serve and love others. Write down strategies for linking the two every time you are tempted to drop your guard. Your love can help you conquer your lack of restraint.

- *Make amends.* When our character is deficient, we usually end up hurting people—sometimes those we care about most. One way to leave old habits behind is to confess our mistakes to those we've offended, offer to make amends, and ask for forgiveness. We know that God places great value on the act of forgiveness: "When you are praying, first forgive anyone you are holding a grudge against, so that your Father in heaven will forgive your sins, too."[20] When you ask, the person you've wronged may not forgive easily, if at all, but God will notice and honor the attempt. In addition, you'll have a greater understanding of how your character affects others.
- *Keep a journal.* When weeks stretch into months, it's easy to forget how much we've grown in our efforts to develop a godly ethos. Keep a written record of your successes as well as your struggles so that you can look back periodically and note how far you've come. You'll be encouraged when you're able to adopt a long-term perspective.
- *Find an accountability partner.* Earlier in this book, I recommended that you enlist another person to hold you accountable as you develop the quality of virtue. You may find it useful, however, to regularly touch base with an accountability partner about your progress on *all* of your character weaknesses. Choose someone who is honest, wise, and encouraging, and you will find the journey a little smoother.

Soaring like an Eagle

The idea of transforming your character into the ethos of God is more than wishful thinking. It is within your grasp—*if* you identify the driving force that will lead you to resemble, reflect, and reveal the character of Christ and *if* you put your trust and your plan in the hands of God. Yes, there will be days when you feel too insignificant and weak to even be worthy of His attention. But don't lose hope! These are the times when He will give you His power and strength so, as Scripture says, you can soar like an eagle:

> He gives power to the weak
> and strength to the powerless.
> Even youths will become weak and tired,
> and young men will fall in exhaustion.
> But those who trust in the LORD will find new strength.
> They will soar high on wings like eagles.[21]

BECOMING YOUR BEST YOU

What weaknesses do you need to turn to strengths?

How might being open with God and others about your struggles help you move forward?

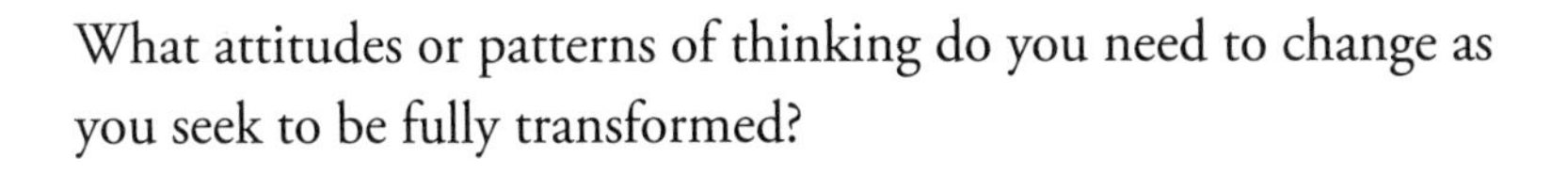

What attitudes or patterns of thinking do you need to change as you seek to be fully transformed?

How can you cultivate a sense of God's presence?

What practical steps will you take to activate God's power in your life?

Dear God, I want to be transformed. I want my character to reflect Yours because I know that's the only way I will be the person You have created me to be. Thank You that this isn't something I need to do alone. Thank You for working in my life every day. Please give me courage and persistence as I seek to change my weaknesses into strengths. Amen.

12

YOUR SUPREME DESTINY

Reflecting the Character of God

The LORD directs the steps of the godly.

PSALM 37:23

WHEN YOU WERE a little girl or boy, did you ever get so excited about an upcoming event that you couldn't sit still? It might have been the final days before Christmas and the anticipation of opening all those colorfully wrapped presents under the tree. Maybe it was a long-awaited visit by your grandparents or favorite uncle. Perhaps it was your first flight on an airplane, the chance to soar into the blue beyond and see the world as you'd never seen it before.

I hope you are that kind of excited right now. I hope that, like a child on her first flight, your view of the world has expanded exponentially. Perhaps for the first time you are picturing the incredible potential of a future that can be yours. The eight secrets we've been discussing are your keys to a life that offers more than you've previously imagined—more joy, more impact, more purpose, more peace. By taking on the ethos of God and making His character your own, you will transform the quality of your existence and enter His best life for you. Not necessarily through wealth, influence, or good health—though certainly all these blessings are more than possible—but through everything that truly matters. You will become the best *you* that you can be.

As you consider this, you may not realize that there's more at stake than what happens to *your* life. The lives of people around the world may be profoundly changed by what you do with your new knowledge of these eight life-altering secrets. Let me explain.

For centuries, so many men and women have misunderstood God's intentions for them. We have interpreted decrees such as the Ten Commandments and other instructions in Scripture to mean that our task in life is to "follow the rules." Many of us have imagined God as a stern taskmaster, concerned only with how well we keep within restrictive boundaries. Yet the commandments, while telling us what not to do, actually serve as a loving invitation to reflect God's character.

We will, of course, benefit from obedience to God. But He desires so much more from us—and *for* us.

You may know the story of a woman caught in bed with a man who wasn't her husband. The religious authorities of the day—men who were all about rules—were frustrated and angered by the Galilean known as Jesus, who taught from a very different perspective. They marched the woman in front of Jesus, hoping to trap Him with her crime.

"Teacher," one said, "this woman was caught in the act of adultery. The law of Moses says to stone her. What do you say?"

To their consternation, Jesus didn't answer. He simply stooped and drew in the dust with His finger. When they pressed Him further, Jesus astonished them with His answer: "All right, but let the one who has never sinned throw the first stone!" One by one, the accusers slinked away.

Jesus isn't only about rules. He is also about grace. He didn't excuse the actions of the woman, but neither did He condemn her. Instead, He simply said, "Go and sin no more."[1]

We often think in a limited, black-and-white way. But God's character is so much more powerful and beautiful than anything we could dream up on our own. And it is only when we begin to think, act, and love like God that we start to appreciate all He has in store for us. His plan for us is that we acquire His character. When we do, and when we submit to the Holy Spirit living in us, He gives us an indescribable, holy power—the ability to change not just our own lives but also those all around us.

One of the great afternoons of my life occurred a few years ago in England. I had the privilege of spending a two-hour car trip with the respected theologian Dr. John Stott. During our conversation, Dr. Stott said to me, "When I get to heaven, one of the things I want to ask God is, 'Why is it that areas of the world where Christianity is so dynamic and vibrant are also breeding grounds for intolerance, hatred, and racism?'"

He pointed out examples from recent history: Northern Ireland, where both Protestants and Catholics were devout in their faith, yet both so often spilled each other's blood; South Africa, where members of the Dutch Reformed Church showed a passionate love for the Lord, yet also provided the theological foundation for apartheid, one of the most racist social systems ever devised; and the American Bible Belt, where for so long many faithful church members seemed to carry a Bible in one hand and a whip for slaves in the other.

The problem has always plagued us. From the Pharisees in biblical times, to the Crusades and Inquisitions in the Middle Ages, to corrupt and quarreling politicians today, we see examples of Christians who have misunderstood God's purposes and abused His name.

Even today's church struggles with this issue. In too many houses of worship, we've lost our perspective. We seem more concerned with attracting people than with teaching them what they need to know. There is nothing wrong with a large congregation. We just need to make sure our focus is less on growing bigger churches and more on growing better people.

The result of our neglect is a body of Christ that does not understand God's ethos. It is a sad commentary on the state of Christianity today, yet it is true that many non-Christians better resemble the character of God—perhaps especially the dimensions of kindness and love—than Christians.

At the time, I did not know how to answer Dr. Stott's question about why so many strongholds of faith seem to be havens for most unholy attitudes and behavior. Now I think I know. It is because we have lost sight of our primary mission. One of Jesus' gifts to the world was communicating and modeling the true character of God. Our task as His followers is not to simply follow the rules. It is to resemble, reflect, and reveal that character so that the world will see God's glory. Our emphasis in the church must be not only on salvation—on first coming to God—but on transformation. Being a follower of Jesus is more than a onetime decision; it's a lifetime of drawing closer to God and letting Him change us. The doctrine that is above all others is to be like Jesus, live like Jesus, and love like Jesus.

I believe we are at a watershed moment in our history. We

face a crisis of character that threatens to undermine everything on earth that God stands for. We need more than ever before to engage His ethos. We need it in our schoolyards, marketplaces, churches, legislative and judicial systems, top leadership rungs of corporate America, and the White House. It is needed by lawyers, doctors, preachers, and teachers, by the mechanics who fix our cars and the cashiers who ring up our purchases. Most of all, we need it at home and in our personal lives.

When people see—*really* see—through us what God is about, they will reach for Him and be changed forever.

This is more than a duty or item to check off on our "to do" list.

This is our supreme destiny.

Divine Life Appointments

Have you ever arrived somewhere at just the right moment to take advantage of a spectacular, unexpected opportunity? Have you ever been faced with a problem and come upon just the right person to help you solve it? You probably marveled because you knew this was not something you had planned or orchestrated. You sensed your steps being directed instead by Someone greater than yourself.

These seeming coincidences are actually golden moments of destiny. You are being guided by an intelligence that is literally out of this world. Such divine life appointments are God-generated gifts that lead to other opportunities—open doors to your specially designed future.

The annals of the past are filled with examples of people who walked through a doorway to their moment of destiny. Abraham Lincoln led our nation through a bitter Civil War and abolished slavery. Winston Churchill inspired steadfast resistance during the bleakest moments of World War II. Martin Luther King Jr. was the face of hope and change during the civil rights movement of the 1950s and 1960s. When the time came, each was prepared to seize his opportunity.

Earlier in your life, you probably missed many of these moments of destiny. You failed to ask for or anticipate them, and you didn't recognize them when they appeared. You overlooked opportunities to achieve greatness because your character was not aligned with God's.

When the foundations of your life begin to consistently reflect the eight pillars of God's ethos, however, your view changes. Before, it was as if you were stumbling about in the dark. Now it's as if you're wearing night-vision goggles. What was inky blackness before is suddenly clear as day. You can both sense and see God's presence in your life, urging you toward wise and holy choices—and toward moments when you can have a profound impact on the world around you.

The apostle Peter acknowledges this at the end of the Bible passage that serves as the foundation for this book. After listing the qualities we need to cultivate to become more like God, he writes, "The more you grow like this, the more productive and useful you will be in your knowledge of our Lord Jesus Christ."[2] Being productive in God's Kingdom means we get the opportunity to change the world for His glory.

Yet even this is not all that God desires for you. Your divine life appointments, your opportunities to impact others, are moments for which you were created, but they are not the *reason* you were created. What you do is of huge importance, but who you are is even more crucial. Your purpose—the reason for your existence—is to grow ever more perfectly to resemble, reflect, and reveal God's character. To fully experience the great life, to be the person you were created to be, you must understand and embrace each of His eight core dimensions. This is what enables us to live like Christ. This is our *supreme* destiny.

Bill Howard is a man who kept a divine life appointment and experienced a taste of his best destiny. Bill was waiting for a plane one day when he noticed a young man whose badly scarred face was obviously the result of a terrible fire. Feeling at once both compassion and repulsion, Bill couldn't help but stare at the man's gruesome appearance.

What Bill didn't know at that moment was that a friend of his had been praying that Bill would have the opportunity to share about the Lord on his flight. God was at work.

A mix-up on the crowded flight left Bill without his assigned seat, and he soon discovered that the disfigured man was in the same predicament. After all the other passengers had been seated, the only open seats remaining were two together in row seven. Bill and the burn victim finally sat down and the flight attendants prepared the cabin for departure.

As the plane taxied down the runway, the young man stared out the window. Bill wanted to talk with him, but what would he say? And what if the man rebuffed him? *I'd feel like a jerk for intruding in his life,* Bill thought.

That was when Bill's *faith* kicked in. He reminded himself that God would be present in the conversation. *Virtue* encouraged him to do the right thing, *wisdom* helped him gather the words to say, and *self-control* gave him the courage to proceed even when he felt apprehensive. *Perseverance* helped him to continue the conversation even when it didn't go perfectly, *sacredness* let him see the holiness of the moment, and *kindness* encouraged him to reach out when it would have been easier to stay detached. Finally, *love* was both his primary motivation and his primary goal. Because he knew of God's amazing love for this man, Bill wanted to share it. He began a conversation.

The man's name was Johnny, and he soon told Bill his story. He and his father had stopped at a gas station while on a road trip. As they stood stretching their legs, a car pulled out in front of a tanker truck on the highway. The truck driver swerved to avoid a collision, but the tanker jackknifed, rolled over, and burst into flames. In an instant, Johnny and his father were covered with burning gasoline.

Bill asked about Johnny's hands. Johnny explained that he had seen an old man at the gas station pinned to the ground by a steel rod as a result of the accident. Johnny had hurried over and lifted the rod, which was red-hot from the flames. That life-saving deed had burned off Johnny's hands.

Over the next three years, Johnny had endured 130 operations, and that summer he was scheduled to receive a pair of artificial hands.

After Johnny finished his story, Bill asked if he'd ever thought about God since the accident. Johnny said he had, but it had never occurred to him that he could have a relationship with the God who had spared his life.

As the plane landed, the two men prayed and Johnny put his faith and trust in Jesus.[3]

On that plane ride, Bill Howard not only stepped through an open door into a divine appointment; he also felt the thrill and fulfillment that comes from grasping our best destiny. At the same time, he helped a new friend along the journey toward faith in the Lord and acquiring the character of Christ.

This is what God imagines for us. *This* is His best life for us.

Do you see yourself as a child of destiny? You should. God has a great future in mind for each and every life, including yours. I searched and dreamed for many years without knowing what I was created for. Yet God was actively pointing me toward Him and His plan for me. With His help, I discovered what I am sure is my purpose.

God is at work in your life, too. Even now He is placing divine life appointments and amazing opportunities in your path. Be careful not to squelch the sense of destiny you feel inside. Don't smother it with negative thoughts and insecurities. Instead, commit yourself to making the journey toward godly character. You will begin to sense the greatness to which God has called you, whether in or out of the spotlight. You will become more hopeful, more confident, more daring, filled with power and purpose, expectant with meaning and significance. Remember, God's very best is His ethos. When His character is in you and lives in you, you will live His best life for you.

Everything is possible when you begin to reflect, resemble, and reveal the character of Christ: belief, virtue, wisdom, self-control, perseverance, sacredness, kindness, and love.

Are you ready? Your future is waiting for you.

Appendix

Your Best Destiny: A Practical Assessment Tool

Do you want to go further in exploring and embracing the character of God? Great! This practical assessment tool is the next step.

Each section of the Your Best Destiny Personal Assessment Tool will enable you to dig deeper into one of the eight core dimensions of God's character. Each contains questions that ask how you might respond in a variety of scenarios. Looking at the questions here will be helpful, but we also encourage you to go to www.YourBestDestinyAssessment.com and use the code provided to take our full assessment and receive feedback. This assessment tool was developed by Dr. William Sedlacek, professor emeritus of education at the University of Maryland and one of the nation's leading authorities on noncognitive assessments. This wonderful tool for growth is designed to help you identify your strengths and launch you into living God's best life for you.

The website will also give you valuable written and visual resources—such as questions, books, sermons, Bible studies, and music—that are related to the eight pillars of character.

As you embark on this journey of self-discovery, I pray that you will keep your focus where it needs to be—on the Creator from whom all blessings flow.

Belief

Childlikeness

Imagine that you are on your lunch break in a park and a few children are playing hide-and-seek with an older sibling. They ask you to join their game. How might you respond to their invitation?

1. Tell them no thanks and focus on my lunch.
2. Join the game after I finish eating and play until my break is over.
3. Tell them no and move to a different, quieter location.
4. Politely decline but watch them have fun.
5. Other: ______________________

Confidence

Let's say you are about to start a big project in your home, and it is something you have never done before. Which best describes how you feel before the project starts?

1. I worry that something will probably go wrong.
2. I'm tired before I have even started.
3. I'm unsure of my ability to reach a satisfactory outcome.
4. I feel confident that I will pull it off because I have always been good at conquering new things.
5. Other: ______________________

Conviction

Consider something that you believe in strongly, such as a political stance, a religious practice, or a child-rearing method. Would you consider it a true conviction? Which best describes your opinion about this belief?

1. I don't expect to have this same belief in the near future.
2. I am open to other ways of thinking about this belief. It's possible that I might change it at some point.
3. I am open to changing my belief, but I feel strongly about it and am unlikely to do so.
4. I am not sure.
5. Other: ______________________

Creativity

Imagine that you work for a company and your boss asks you to come up with a new slogan and design for the company's website. How might you feel about this?

1. Worried and anxious.
2. Excited about the opportunity.
3. Overwhelmed by such a big task.
4. Sure that I will need help to do it.
5. Other: ______________________

Energy

Loyalty to favorite sports teams is a form of belief that stimulates action. If you attend sporting events to follow your favorite team, what type of fan would you say you are?

1. Always calm, cool, and collected.
2. Often anxious and tense.
3. Lively and animated.
4. Irate and agitated, to the point of yelling and screaming most of the time.
5. Other: ______________________

Happiness

Consider how you have felt emotionally over the past week or two. Did your happiness stem from a belief that was affirmed? Which of these statements best describes how you felt?

1. Joyful and content.
2. Tired and worn down.
3. Anxious and tense.
4. Up and down; I had a mixture of feelings from gloomy to satisfied.
5. Other: ______________________

Hopefulness

Let's say yesterday was one of those days when everything seemed to go wrong. Which of these statements describes how you feel?

1. Tired of trying.
2. Depressed.
3. Confident that tomorrow will be better.
4. Puzzled as to why things went wrong.
5. Other: ______________________

Inspiration

How would you feel if you were attending your annual company meeting and, during a break, your boss asked you to give one hundred of your colleagues a five-minute speech to get them energized and excited about the upcoming year?

1. Nervous to the point of freezing up.
2. Pumped up with adrenaline and filled with ideas.
3. Calm and clear-headed.

4. Willing to comply but aware that I might not be well received.
5. Other: ______________________

Optimism

When you were in school, you took many tests and exams. Imagine that you have just completed a test that was harder than you expected it to be. How might you feel about it?

1. As if I probably failed.
2. Angry at the teacher for making the test so hard.
3. Cautiously confident and hopeful that I was able to "pull it out of the fire."
4. So nervous and jittery about the outcome that it's hard to stop thinking about it.
5. Other: ______________________

What have you learned from these questions? Are you ready to take belief to a new level in your life? Is faith a strength or weakness of your ethos?

Virtue

Honesty

How do you feel about the phrase "honesty is the best policy"?

1. I completely agree with it. People should be honest no matter what.
2. I agree with it in principle, but I know that lying once in a while is just a fact of life.
3. I view this advice as completely unrealistic.
4. I believe that lying is okay as long as it doesn't hurt anyone.
5. Other: ______________________

Modesty

Imagine that you are involved in a group project at work. You feel that you have done most of the work, but everyone in the group will get the same credit. What is your response?

1. I will be sure to let my boss know about my substantial contribution.
2. I will try to persuade my coworkers to give me most of the credit.
3. I will be content knowing that the job was well done.
4. I will avoid working in that group again.
5. Other: ______________________

Morality

Imagine that you have a friend who seems to decide what is right or wrong depending on the circumstances and his own set of guiding principles. How do you feel about that?

1. I think this approach seems simplistic.
2. I think my friend has the right idea.
3. I always check with someone else about what is right or wrong.
4. Who is to say what is right or wrong?
5. Other: ______________________

Nobility

Let's say that on a number of occasions you have helped your extended family members with your money and time, but they have never helped you. Now a cousin needs some help with a problem. What will you do?

1. Say that I have helped enough and it's someone else's turn.
2. Do my best to help him since I may be the only one who can.
3. Try to avoid talking to him.
4. Tell him that I'm burned out and need help myself.
5. Other: ______________________

Obedience

Imagine that you decide to take a class at a local community college. At the first session, the professor lists a number of class rules that you don't agree with, such as not allowing the use of computers or cell phones. What will you do?

1. Discuss the rules with the professor.
2. Accept the rules.
3. Try to use my computer and/or cell phone anyway, while being careful not to disrupt the class or draw attention to myself.

4. Drop the class.
5. Other: ______________________

Prudence

Imagine that at the end of the year your boss unexpectedly tells you that you will be getting a large bonus check. What will you most likely do with the money?

1. Spend it on a vacation.
2. Throw a big party to celebrate.
3. Save it.
4. Put it toward a big-ticket item such as a car.
5. Other: ______________________

Purity

Many religious groups are advocates for purity, recommending that their members stay away from things like alcohol, drugs, and premarital sex. How do you feel about this?

1. Everyone should behave this way. No exceptions.
2. I mostly agree with these principles, but I don't think rules can be pasted over impure hearts.
3. I agree that too many of these things are not good, but I think everything is okay in moderation.
4. I disagree with religious groups that have this stance.
5. Other: ______________________

Selflessness

We describe individuals as selfless when they put other people's wants and needs above their own. How well do you feel that you match this description?

1. I can be selfless at times, but frankly, I am usually concerned with my own well-being.
2. I do not consider myself to be selfless at all.
3. I would consider myself to be a selfless person, but not 100 percent of the time.
4. I am the most selfless person I know.
5. Other: ______________________

Sincerity

You have a friend who always tells the truth no matter what the consequences. How do you feel about this?

1. I sometimes feel I need to tell a white lie to protect someone's feelings.
2. I simply try to do the same as my friend.
3. My friend makes me feel uncomfortable.
4. I feel this is impractical and that the truth should be expressed in different ways depending on the circumstances.
5. Other: ______________________

Did you recognize any trouble spots? Were you able to identify weaknesses in the wall that protects and purifies your mind? If you are finding it difficult to stand up to temptation or control your negative thoughts, there is a reason, and you can't properly fortify your heart and mind until you know what that reason is. Real joy begins when you cultivate what virtue reveals to your heart and soul.

Wisdom

Earnestness

Think about times when you have been in a work setting. Which statement best reflects how your colleagues would describe your work style?

1. Serious and purposeful.
2. Funny and lighthearted.
3. Laid back and reserved.
4. Energetic and talkative.
5. Other: ______________________

Efficiency

Think back to a day in your life when you had a large number of tasks to complete. How did you respond?

1. I felt overwhelmed.
2. I accomplished everything but was worn out afterward.
3. I realized I couldn't do it all and just did what I could.
4. I figured out creative ways to get things done without becoming burned out.
5. Other: ______________________

Fearlessness

Your friend tells you he is going to bungee jump off a bridge and wants you to join him. What might you do?

1. Enthusiastically say yes.
2. Think about it for a while but then probably decide to do it.
3. Tell him no without hesitation.

4. Offer to go with him and make up my mind after I see the bridge.
5. Other: ______________________

Initiative

Imagine that over the past few years crime in your neighborhood has increased and that the area in general has become more rundown. What might you do about this?

1. Try to move someplace new.
2. Talk about it with a friend.
3. Form a group to take action.
4. Write to my local politician.
5. Other: ______________________

Persistence

Imagine that for several weeks you have been trying to stop a door in your house from squeaking. Despite your efforts, it still squeaks. What will you do now?

1. Give up. I have better things to do.
2. Ask my neighbor to help me correct the problem.
3. Keep trying things until it stops squeaking.
4. Call a repair person.
5. Other: ______________________

Purpose

Some people seem to live a life of purpose, guided by a few select principles that they strongly adhere to no matter what their situation. How do you feel you compare to these types of people?

1. I am nothing like those people.
2. I am currently searching for purpose in my life.

3. I am exactly like one of those people.
4. I have purpose in my life, but I don't think much about it.
5. Other: ______________________

Resiliency

Think about times in your life when a friendship or romantic relationship has ended. How do you usually react when this occurs?

1. I feel sad for a short period of time, but I am able to move on fairly quickly.
2. I get over it immediately.
3. I take a long time to recover from the loss, but eventually I do.
4. I have difficulty ever recovering.
5. Other: ______________________

Responsibility

Let's say you make a mistake at work that costs your employer money. There is no way, however, that anyone will know it was your mistake. What will you do?

1. Keep quiet and hope for the best.
2. Own up to the mistake with my boss.
3. Keep quiet and begin to look for another job.
4. Tell my family but no one else.
5. Other: ______________________

Thoroughness

You are cleaning out your garage and you find many boxes. You could look through the contents before throwing them out, but that would make the job take much longer than you want it to.

What would you do?

1. Throw out the boxes after a quick check of their contents.
2. Carefully go through the contents of each box.
3. Try to get someone else to check the contents of the boxes.
4. Put off the job until I have more time to check the contents of the boxes.
5. Other: ______________________

Are you feeling more or less wise after taking this quiz? Have the questions helped you identify a quality of character you need to develop further?

Self-Control

Decisiveness

Suppose your nine-year-old daughter asks whether she can go on an overnight trip with friends. Which best describes your reaction?

1. You think about it for a long period of time and then make a decision.
2. You consult a close friend or family member for advice.
3. You avoid giving her an answer.
4. You think about it briefly and then make a decision without consulting anyone.
5. Other: ______________________

Determination

Let's say that you have the goal to run a marathon but have failed twice to reach the end of the race. Now, on your third try, you come up short again. What best describes what you would do next?

1. Train even harder and try a fourth time.
2. Give up running altogether.
3. Switch your goal to a half marathon.
4. Ask for advice.
5. Other: ______________________

Discipline

Imagine that your doctor tells you that for health reasons you must not eat chocolate for the next year. Chocolate, however, is your all-time favorite food. What would you likely do in this situation?

1. Get a second opinion from another doctor.
2. Stay off chocolate for a few days, then eat only a little bit every day.
3. Go home and eat some chocolate.
4. Stay committed to avoiding chocolate.
5. Other: ______________________

Integrity

If you volunteered to serve at a community picnic but then were offered tickets to a football game with your favorite team on the same day, what would you do?

1. Go to the game and fail to show up at the picnic.
2. Stick to your word and go to the picnic.
3. Say you are not feeling well to get out of the picnic and go to the game.
4. Go to the picnic, but ask if you can leave early to catch some of the game.
5. Other: ______________________

Maturity

Think about the person you were at age fourteen and who you are today. Which sentence below best describes what comes to mind?

1. I am pretty much the same now as I was then.
2. I make better decisions about my life now than I did then.
3. I made better decisions about my life when I was fourteen than I do now.
4. I don't think much about how I have changed.
5. Other: ______________________

Sacrifice

If your husband or wife were offered a dream job that would require moving away from friends and family and a job that you enjoy, what might be your reaction?

1. Try to persuade your husband or wife to stay where you are.
2. Tell your spouse that you won't move, no matter what.
3. Happily sacrifice what you have in your current location for your husband or wife.
4. Follow your spouse but feel bitter and unhappy about it.
5. Other: ______________________

Steadfastness

Imagine you are running a restaurant that has been successful for years. Recently, however, business has declined. What might you do in this situation?

1. Change your staff.
2. Change your menu.
3. Keep things the same for the next few months.
4. Close the business.
5. Other: ______________________

Strength

You just found out that a close family member has an incurable disease. Which option would best describe your reaction?

1. You worry that you may have the same disease.
2. You call upon your inner resources to deal with it.
3. You try to learn the facts about the disease.
4. You try not to think about it.
5. Other: ______________________

Temperance

Suppose that peanut M&M'S are your favorite candy and someone gives you a big bag of them for your birthday. What would you do with the candy?

1. Give it away so you won't be tempted to eat too much.
2. Eat until you are completely full.
3. Eat as much as you can, even after you get full.
4. Eat some each day over a long period of time.
5. Other: ______________________

How did you measure up? Is self-control bringing balance to your life and character?

Perseverance

Cooperation

Let's say that a big job needs to be done at work, one that requires perseverance. You have to figure out how to accomplish it. Would you prefer to

1. work on it alone until it gets finished?
2. form a team to do it together, where all have equal leadership?
3. form a team on which you will decide what each person does?
4. form a team and ask someone else to take the lead?
5. Other: ______________________

Diplomacy

Suppose that two of your close friends get into a fight and ask you to help them decide who was right and who was wrong. Would you

1. ask them not to drag you into it?
2. encourage them to figure it out themselves?
3. have them tell you the problem, and then you decide who is right?
4. help them figure out a compromise?
5. Other: ______________________

Fellowship

Imagine that you move to a new part of the country where you don't know anyone. What would you do first?

1. Join a church or activity group where you would meet and be around many people.
2. Try to make friends with people where you work.
3. Go out to restaurants and bars frequently and introduce yourself to others.
4. Keep to yourself unless you happen to meet people.
5. Other: ______________________

Flexibility

What if you had been planning a special vacation for months but a continuous rainstorm on the first day ruined your plans. How would you feel?

1. Angry and frustrated.
2. Sad that things fell through.
3. Sad for a moment, but then happy to do something different.
4. Upset and thinking that "things never seem to work out for me."
5. Other: ______________________

Hospitality

Pretend that a new family is moving in next door to you today. What will you do?

1. Wait to see what they are like.
2. Invite them over for a meal.
3. Watch them from the window as they move in.
4. Hope they don't make a lot of noise.
5. Other: ______________________

Patience

Let's say you go to renew your driver's license and are told that the wait will be twenty minutes. An hour later, with no signs of headway, how would you feel?

1. Angry.
2. Anxious.
3. Calm.
4. Annoyed.
5. Other: ______________________

Tact

Imagine that you meet your daughter's date for the evening for the first time. He has a number of tattoos that look obscene to you. Would you

1. confront him about the tattoos?
2. forbid your daughter to go out with him?
3. talk to him to try to figure out what he's like?
4. avoid dealing with him?
5. Other: ______________________

Thoughtfulness

You are in a hurry to get to an appointment. On the street you pass your neighbor, who seems very upset. What will you do?

1. Stop and ask him how he feels and if there is anything you can do to help.
2. Be pleasant, but hurry on to your appointment.
3. Nod to him and pretend you don't notice he's upset.
4. Assume that we all have bad days sometimes and move on.
5. Other: ______________________

Tolerance

Imagine that your uncle has political views much different from yours—and he is always telling you about them. Would you

1. avoid him?
2. listen to his views and share your own?
3. tell him to shut up?
4. allow him to talk, but refuse to listen?
5. Other: ________________________

What do your quiz answers tell you about your patience and ability to persevere? Did anything surprise you?

Sacredness

Adoration

You're at a football game and the crowd around you erupts in applause and cheers when the home team players take the field. How do you feel about fans who practically worship athletes?

1. Sports are a fun and harmless diversion.
2. It's fine to root for the home team but best to keep sports in perspective.
3. Great players deserve all the adulation they receive.
4. Hero worship of athletes has gone too far.
5. Other: ______________________

Awe

You're watching a winter storm from the window of your beachfront hotel. Suddenly an enormous wave washes onshore, nearly reaching the hotel. What is your response?

1. Relief that you're inside instead of on the beach.
2. Wonder at the forces that combine to power such a wall of water.
3. Worry about when the next wave will hit.
4. Total fear.
5. Other: ______________________

Holiness

Let's say that one of your church leaders seems very devout and holy. How would you compare yourself to that person?

1. I, too, am an extremely holy person.
2. I consider myself to be holy, but not overly so.

3. I am striving to be more holy in my life. It is a work in progress.
4. I do not consider myself to be holy in the least.
5. Other: ______________________

Humility

Imagine that you have been a community leader for many years without being noticed by others. Just recently you received an award for all your hard work. How would you react?

1. Feel like I deserved it for all the work I put in.
2. Have the award framed and hung in my living room.
3. Tell those close to me about the award.
4. Nothing special; I did it for the community.
5. Other: ______________________

Piety

You've always seen yourself as devoted to your faith. Your new neighbor informs you that he attends church every night of the week. You feel

1. admiration for his dedication.
2. inspired to go to church more yourself.
3. irritation that your neighbor seems to be bragging.
4. secure in your own faith habits.
5. Other: ______________________

Respect

Imagine that you work at a coffee shop and a man wearing a military uniform walks in. How might you talk to him?

1. Just like anyone else.
2. With a high level of admiration.

3. With contempt.
4. With great enthusiasm.
5. Other: ______________________

Reverence

Imagine that you take trip to Washington, DC, where you visit the Vietnam Veterans Memorial. Here on a large wall are inscribed the names of all the soldiers who died in the Vietnam War. How do you imagine you would feel as you visit the site?

1. A deep level of respect and honor for those who died.
2. Probably boredom. It's just a wall and not much else.
3. Not sure I would feel anything. I don't know anyone listed on the wall.
4. Probably would feel uncomfortable thinking about all those who died.
5. Other: ______________________

Righteousness

Imagine that one night you are walking in the city with a group of friends and one of your friends, as a joke, decides to pick up a rock and throw it at a parked car, smashing the windshield. What would you do?

1. I would just keep walking with the group.
2. I would tell my friend that his action was stupid and walk away from the group.
3. I would demand that my friend figure out a way to pay for the damage he caused.
4. I would laugh along with my friend.
5. Other: ______________________

Truth

How do you respond to this biblical proverb: "Truthful words stand the test of time, but lies are soon exposed" (Proverbs 12:19)?

1. I have seen how lies stay buried and liars get away with lying.
2. When I have spoken truth, I have never regretted it.
3. I would rather suffer in the present for truth than suffer later for lying.
4. It's too hard to tell the difference between truth and falsehood.
5. Other: ________________________

Have you learned more about your attitudes toward the holy and sacred? Do you have anything in mind that you want to change?

Kindness

Benevolence

As you enter the grocery store, you pass by a volunteer asking for donations to help those who have lost their jobs and homes due to a recent hurricane. Choose which best describes what you would do.

1. Say you are sorry but not give any money.
2. Make an excuse that you do not have money right now.
3. Make a donation and thank the volunteer for his effort.
4. Try to go in another door to avoid having to talk to this person.
5. Other: ________________________

Cheerfulness

You have a day where your child is sick, you have a job you don't like, and you are short of food in the house. Choose which best describes how you would feel.

1. Depressed over the situation.
2. Hopeful that things will someday change.
3. Optimistic that you'll feel better tomorrow.
4. Angry about your plight.
5. Other: ________________________

Compassion

You are late for work. On your commute you see a dog that looks hurt lying by the side of the road. Choose which best describes what you would do.

1. Drive on. It is not your dog so it does not concern you.
2. Stop and try to help the dog.

3. Stop and look for others who can help you with the dog.
4. Call 911.
5. Other: ______________________

Fairness

Imagine that a religious group that you do not support is planning on building a place of worship in your neighborhood. What would you do?

1. Organize an effort to keep it from being built.
2. Talk with your friends and family about how much you disapprove of it.
3. Nothing.
4. Welcome them.
5. Other: ______________________

Generosity

After the Hurricane Katrina disaster, many organizations asked for donations to help those in need. What did you do at that time?

1. Made a donation.
2. Gave no money at all. I didn't feel it was that important.
3. Gave no money at all. I was really struggling at the time myself.
4. Thought about it but did not make a donation.
5. Other: ______________________

Gentleness

Think about the people who know you best. Which of the following best captures how they would describe your personality?

1. Good sense of humor.
2. Compassionate when someone has a need.
3. Always going to social events.
4. Serious and constantly working.
5. Other: ______________________

Gratitude

Imagine that you are struggling to make ends meet and can't pay the rent. A person from work overhears this, and he pays your rent without asking for anything in return. What might you do in this situation?

1. Nothing. You didn't ask him to do it.
2. Wonder what he wants out of it.
3. Tell him "Thank you."
4. Write him a thank-you note describing what the act meant to you.
5. Other: ______________________

Respect

Imagine that you are at the post office and a uniformed police officer walks in. How might you talk to this person?

1. Just like anyone else.
2. With a high level of admiration.
3. With contempt.
4. With great enthusiasm.
5. Other: ______________________

Sympathy

Imagine that a neighbor has a learning disability and has difficulty expressing herself. How might you feel about this?

1. Be glad that it's not you.
2. Want to offer to speak for her.
3. Feel compassion for her.
4. Want to avoid her.
5. Other: ______________________

What do your quiz answers tell you about your level of kindness?

Love

Affection

A new friend asks how often you express affection. What would you tell her?

1. I am like most people, fairly average.
2. Very little. I am not a "touchy-feely" person.
3. I express affection with those close to me.
4. I express a lot of affection with all the people in my life.
5. Other: ____________________

Attentiveness

Imagine that you are walking in the parking lot of a grocery store and notice an elderly man struggling to put his grocery bags in his car. What would you do?

1. Nothing. I wouldn't want to offend him.
2. Go over and ask if he wants help.
3. Look to see if someone is around to help him.
4. Help him immediately without asking if he needs it.
5. Other: ____________________

Availability

Imagine that you are a member of a church and your pastor asks you if you would be willing to be "on call" three nights a week in case another church member has an emergency. What would you do?

1. Say you are 100 percent ready and willing to help out.
2. Consult with your family and friends before deciding.
3. Ask if you could do just one or two nights a week.

4. Make up an excuse why you couldn't do this.
5. Other: ______________________

Commitment

You have previously agreed to help a friend move his household belongings, but at the last minute your boss wants you to do extra work that weekend. You can't do both. What would you do?

1. Honor the promise to your friend and explain it to your boss.
2. Explain to your friend that you can't help him because of work.
3. Tell your boss you are sick and can't work.
4. Tell your friend you are sick and can't help him.
5. Other: ______________________

Dependability

You have promised your neighbors to recruit some people to help clean up a playground by a certain date. What would you do?

1. The best I could.
2. Not take the deadline as an exact date.
3. Make sure I did what I said I would do.
4. It's volunteer work, so I would be flexible.
5. Other: ______________________

Encouragement

A youngster in the neighborhood is trying to build a house for his dog and is having a difficult time of it. What would you do?

1. Tell him that it is a tough job and he should get help.
2. Tell him to forget it; it's too much work for him.
3. Encourage him to stick with it.

4. Step in and build it for him.
5. Other: ______________________

Ingenuity

Imagine that you are on a television game show and you are part of a team given the task of solving a big puzzle that requires creativity and resourcefulness. What kind of team member might you be?

1. The leader. I am great at coming up with ideas.
2. An involved helper. I might be able to add something useful.
3. A helper that does only what the leader suggests.
4. Someone who tries to stay completely on the sidelines.
5. Other: ______________________

Security

Imagine that a close member of your family has a serious accident and asks you to take care of his two children while he is recovering. How might you react to this?

1. Accept the task, but with fear and anxiety.
2. Accept the task, treating it like a challenge.
3. See if there is someone else who can do it.
4. Easily accept the task. I am used to taking care of others.
5. Other: ______________________

Sensitivity

Think about moments in your life when someone looks emotional but has yet to tell you what they are feeling. In these situations, you usually

1. have a pretty good guess what they are feeling.
2. don't know what they are feeling until they tell me.

3. most often think they are feeling something they are not.
4. don't think about it.
5. Other: ________________________

How did your answers turn out? Did they give you any insights into your character when it comes to love?

Notes

CHAPTER 1: DISCOVERING YOUR BEST DESTINY

1. Clayborne Carson, ed., *The Autobiography of Martin Luther King, Jr.* (New York: Warner, 1998), 9–10.
2. Randy Alcorn, *The Treasure Principle* (Sisters, OR: Multnomah, 2001), 51.
3. Ibid., 50.
4. Helen Kirwan-Taylor, "Miserable? Bored? You Must Be Rich," *The Telegraph,* November 13, 2007, www.telegraph.co.uk/news/features/3634620/Miserable-Bored-You-must-be-rich.html.
5. Ibid.
6. Colossians 1:15, MSG.
7. Luke 16:15, CEV.

CHAPTER 2: YOU ARE A MASTERPIECE

1. Huffington Post, "Meryl Streep Barnard Graduation: 'You Just Have to Make Your Mother and Father Proud,'" May 18, 2010, www.huffingtonpost.com/2010/05/18/meryl-streep-barnard-grad_n_580335.html.
2. http://www.nytimes.com/2009/05/13/us/politics/13obama.text.html?pagewanted=all.
3. Donald R. Keough, *The Ten Commandments for Business Failure* (New York: Portfolio, 2008), 68.
4. Marisa Handler, *Loyal to the Sky* (San Francisco, Berrett-Koehler, 2007), 87.
5. 1 Samuel 16:7.
6. Mark 7:20-23, MSG.
7. Luke 6:45.
8. Jim Daly, *Stronger* (Colorado Springs: David C. Cook, 2010), 176–177.
9. Genesis 1:27.
10. Jeremiah 18:1-6.

11. Ephesians 5:1.
12. Some of my thinking about this passage was influenced by the writing of Ellen G. White, who was a prolific Christian writer and teacher in the nineteenth century.
13. 2 Peter 1:3-4.
14. 2 Peter 1:5-8, emphasis added.

CHAPTER 3: THE POWER OF BELIEF

1. "Self-Fulfilling Prophecy—The Heather Stepp Story," the Georgia Bulldogs women's gymnastics team website, accessed October 30, 2014, http://www.georgiadogs.com/sports/w-gym/spec-rel/111209aab.html. See also "Stepp McCormick New Member of Georgia Sports HOF," the Georgia Bulldogs women's gymnastics team website, February 23, 2013, www.georgiadogs.com/sports/w-gym/spec-rel/022313aaa.html.
2. Herbert Benson, *Timeless Healing* (New York: Scribner, 1996), 61.
3. Bruce H. Lipton, *The Biology of Belief* (Carlsbad, CA: Hay House, 2008), 139–140.
4. Hebrews 11:1.
5. John 20:25.
6. John 20:27-29.
7. Matthew 9:27-29, NIV.
8. Matthew 9:29, MSG.
9. Psalm 139:13-14.
10. Patrick Morley, *The Man in the Mirror* (Grand Rapids: Zondervan, 1997), 116–117.
11. Jeremiah 29:11.
12. Ephesians 2:10.
13. Philippians 1:6, MSG.
14. Mark 9:14-24.
15. Ephesians 3:20.
16. Barry C. Black, *From the Hood to the Hill* (Nashville: Thomas Nelson, 2006), 8.

CHAPTER 4: THE BEAUTY OF VIRTUE

1. "The Ethics of American Youth: 2010," Josephson Institute, Center for Youth Ethics, survey report, February 10, 2011, http://charactercounts.org/programs/reportcard/2010/installment02_report-card_honesty-integrity.html, as adapted from Brenda Hunter and Kristen Blair, *From Santa to Sexting* (Abilene, TX: Leafwood, 2012), 217–18.
2. C. S. Lewis, *The Abolition of Man* (New York: HarperCollins, 1944), 24.
3. Vigen Guroian, *Tending the Heart of Virtue* (New York: Oxford University, 1998), 4.
4. Matthew 26:59.
5. John 8:46.
6. John 18:38.
7. Hebrews 4:15.
8. Matthew 23:27.

9. 2 Samuel 11:2-27; 12:1-18.
10. Dennis M. Kizziar, *Fallen, Broken, Restored* (Bend, OR: Maverick, 2013), 14–15.
11. Ephesians 5:3, NIV, emphasis added.
12. Randy Alcorn, *The Purity Principle* (Sisters, OR: Multnomah, 2003), 9–10.
13. 1 Corinthians 10:13.
14. Habakkuk 2:4, ESV.
15. Adapted from Max Lucado, *Grace* (Nashville: Thomas Nelson, 2012), 23–25.
16. 1 John 1:9.
17. Philippians 4:8.
18. Genesis 39; 41:43-45.
19. Noel M. Tichy and Warren G. Bennis, *Judgment: How Winning Leaders Make Great Calls* (New York: Portfolio, 2007), as adapted from Jeremy Kingsley, *Inspired People Produce Results* (New York: McGraw-Hill, 2013), 134–135.
20. John Piper, *Future Grace* (Nashville: Thomas Nelson, 2012), 23–25.

CHAPTER 5: THE JOY OF WISDOM

1. Patsy G. Lovell, "Love Wins," *Focus on the Family* 1993, as adapted from Dr. James & Shirley Dobson, *Night Light for Parents* (Sisters, OR: Multnomah, 2002), 126–127.
2. *Merriam-Webster's Collegiate Dictionary* (Springfield, MA: Merriam-Webster, 1997), 1,358.
3. Proverbs 13:16, NKJV.
4. Proverbs 12:1, NKJV.
5. Proverbs 17:27, NKJV.
6. Black History Web, "19 George Washington Carver Quotes," www.blackistoryweb.info/2013/03/19-george-washington-carver-quotes.html.
7. 1 Kings 3:16-28.
8. 2 Chronicles 1:7-12.
9. 1 Corinthians 3:19.
10. Proverbs 3:13-18.

CHAPTER 6: THE STRENGTH OF SELF-CONTROL

1. Daniel Akst, *We Have Met the Enemy* (New York: Penguin, 2011), 2.
2. Ibid., 6.
3. W. Mischel, Y. Shoda, and M. L. Rodriguez, "Delay of Gratification in Children," *Science* 244 (1989), 933–938, as adapted from Madeleine Levine, *Teach Your Children Well* (New York: HarperCollins, 2012), 221–222.
4. Roy F. Baumeister and John Tierney, *Willpower* (New York: Penguin, 2008), 208.
5. Genesis 1:3.
6. Genesis 1:11.
7. Genesis 1:28.
8. Genesis 1:31.
9. Matthew 16:24, MSG.

10. Hiroo Onoda, *No Surrender* (Tokyo: Kodansha International, 1974), 14, as quoted in Jim Daly and James Lund, *Stronger: Trading Brokenness for Unbreakable Strength* (Colorado Springs: David C. Cook, 2010), 78.
11. Tim Brown, *The Making of a Man* (Nashville: Thomas Nelson, 2014), 201–202.
12. Nancy Leigh DeMoss, *Brokenness, Surrender, Holiness* (Chicago: Moody, 2008), 156.
13. Ibid.

CHAPTER 7: THE PROMISE OF PERSEVERANCE

1. Stormie Omartian, *The Power of a Praying Wife* (Eugene, OR: Harvest House, 1997), 16–17, and Stormie Omartian, *The Power of a Praying Husband* (Eugene, OR: Harvest House, 2001), 18, 21–22.
2. James 1:2-4, NIV.
3. Annie Dillard, *Teaching a Stone to Talk* (New York: Harper Perennial, 2013).
4. Romans 5:3-4, NIV.
5. Adapted from Peb Jackson and James Lund, *Danger Calling* (Grand Rapids: Revell, 2010), 87–93.
6. Luke 18:1.
7. John Maxwell, *The 360-Degree Leader* (Nashville: Thomas Nelson, 2005).
8. Hebrews 10:35-36.

CHAPTER 8: THE GLORY OF SACREDNESS

1. Ron Mehl, *The Tender Commandments* (Sisters, OR: Multnomah, 1998), 87–88.
2. Deuteronomy 5:11.
3. "Brother Lawrence," *Christianity Today*, August 8, 2008, www.christianitytoday .com/ch/131christians/innertravelers/brotherlawrence.html.
4. Nancy Jo Sullivan, *Moments of Grace* (Sisters, OR: Multnomah, 2000), 43–45.
5. Isaiah 6:3, NIV.
6. 1 Peter 1:15-16.
7. Abraham Heschel, *Between God and Man* (New York: Free Press, 1959), 52.
8. 1 Corinthians 3:16-17, NIV.
9. Isaiah 52:11, NIV.
10. Psalm 51:6, CEV.

CHAPTER 9: THE PRACTICE OF KINDNESS

1. Allison Klein, "A Gate-Crasher's Change of Heart," *Washington Post*, July 13, 2007, www.washingtonpost.com/wp-dyn/content/article/2007/07/12/AR2007 071202356.html.
2. Adam Phillips and Barbara Taylor, *On Kindness* (New York: Farrar, Straus, and Giroux, 2009), 16–17.
3. Ibid., 18.
4. "Colorado Boy, 6, Suspended for Kiss Gets Allegations on Record Changed from 'Sexual Harassment' to 'Misconduct,'" *FoxNews*, December 11, 2013,

www.foxnews.com/us/2013/12/11/colorado-school-district-flooded-with-calls-after-6-year-old-suspension-over.
5. e. e. cummings, *Selected Poems* (New York: Grove, 1994), 73.
6. Matthew 7:12.
7. William F. Baker and Michael O'Malley, *Leading with Kindness* (New York: AMACOM, 2008), 24.
8. Jeremy Kingsley, *Inspired People Produce Results* (New York: McGraw-Hill, 2013), 82.
9. Joe Nocera, "Put Buyers First? What a Concept," *New York Times,* January 5, 2008, www.nytimes.com/2008/01/05/technology/05nocera.html?pagewanted=all&_r=0.
10. Luke 10:30-35.
11. Matthew 25:35-40.
12. Kingsley, 74.
13. Emily Dickinson, "If I Can Stop One Heart from Breaking," Bartleby.com, accessed December 20, 2013, www.bartleby.com/113/1006.html.

CHAPTER 10: THE SPLENDOR OF LOVE

1. Genesis 28:10-17.
2. 1 John 4:8.
3. 1 Corinthians 13:1-7, 13.
4. Richard Stengel, *Mandela's Way* (New York: Crown, 2009), 198.
5. 2 Samuel 9.
6. "Magic Johnson and Larry Bird Recall Johnson's HIV Announcement on 'Late Show with David Letterman,'" *Huffington Post,* April 12, 2012, www.huffingtonpost.com/2012/04/12/larry-bird-recalls-magic-johnson-hiv-announcement-video_n_1419903.html.
7. 1 John 4:11-12.
8. Sara Patterson, "Veterans Revisit Pacific for Date with World War II Memories," *Commercial Appeal,* May 28, 2012, www.commercialappeal.com/news/2012/may/28/memorial/?print=1.

CHAPTER 11: A PRESCRIPTION FOR TRANSFORMATION

1. 2 Corinthians 12:7-10.
2. Nancy Leigh DeMoss, *Brokenness, Surrender, Holiness* (Chicago: Moody, 2008), 47.
3. Ibid., 48.
4. 1 Corinthians 11:28-29.
5. Kimberly Rooney, *Spiritual Two-By-Fours and Other Wake-Up Calls* (Bloomington, IN: Balboa, 2013), 172.
6. Psalm 32:3-5.
7. Philippians 4:6, NIV.
8. John 15:5.
9. Psalm 34:18.
10. Romans 12:2.

11. John 15:7, NIV.
12. 1 Chronicles 16:29.
13. Psalm 46:10.
14. John Stott, *Basic Christianity* (Nottingham, UK: InterVarsity, 1958, 1971, 2008), 123.
15. www.brainyquote.com/quotes/quotes/m/michaeljor167381.html.
16. Nehemiah 2:20.
17. Nehemiah 4:14.
18. Nehemiah 6:15.
19. Philippians 4:13.
20. Mark 11:25.
21. Isaiah 40:29-31.

CHAPTER 12: YOUR SUPREME DESTINY

1. John 8:1-11.
2. 2 Peter 1:5-8.
3. Adapted from Dennis Rainey, "Divine Appointments: Are You Listening to the Nudge of the Holy Spirit to Talk to Those around You?" *Family Life*, 2006, www.familylife.com/articles/topics/faith/essentials/reaching-out/divine-appointments#.UtdL7f2A05c.

About the Authors

Wintley Phipps is a world-renowned vocal artist, education activist, motivational speaker, pastor, and CEO and founder of the US Dream Academy. For his work at the US Dream Academy he has received numerous service awards, including *The Excellence in Mentoring for Program Leadership Award* from MENTOR/National Mentoring Partnerships; the Oprah Winfrey Angel Network *Use Your Life Award*; and the *Philanthropist of the Year Award* from the National Center for Black Philanthropy, Inc.

For more than twenty-eight years, Wintley has traveled the world delivering messages of hope, advocacy, and equality to many thousands of people. A video of him performing "Amazing Grace" has enjoyed over seven million views on YouTube. He sang that same song at the 56th Inaugural Presidential Prayer Service on January 21, 2009.

A two-time Grammy Award nominee, Wintley is no stranger to performing in front of distinguished audiences. In addition to President Barack Obama, other notable listeners have included former Presidents Jimmy Carter, Ronald Reagan, George H. W. Bush, Bill Clinton, George W. Bush, former South African President

Nelson Mandela, Mother Teresa of Calcutta, and Oprah Winfrey. Wintley is also an internationally recognized speaker on behalf of the Dream Academy and young people, having completed speaking engagements in Europe, Australia, Asia, Africa, and North and South America. In recognition of his positive global impact through speaking, the National Speakers Association awarded Wintley the prestigious *Master of Influence Award.*

Born in the Republic of Trinidad and Tobago, Wintley moved to Montreal at an early age and then studied at Oakwood University in Huntsville, Alabama, where he received his bachelor of arts degree in theology. He went on to earn a master of divinity from Andrews University in Berrien Springs, Michigan. Wintley has three sons with his wife, Linda Diane Galloway Phipps, and he currently serves as the senior pastor for the Palm Bay Seventh-Day Adventist Church in Palm Bay, Florida.

James Lund is an award-winning writer and editor who frequently works with bestselling authors, public figures, and ministry leaders. He lives in central Oregon with his wife, Angela, and their family. Visit his website: www.jameslundbooks.com.

About the Assessment

THE YOUR BEST DESTINY PERSONAL ASSESSMENT TOOL is based on the work of Dr. William Sedlacek, professor emeritus of the University of Maryland, and Dr. Ryan Duffy, professor at the University of Florida. Much of the work was informed by Dr. Sedlacek's book *Beyond the Big Test: Noncognitive Assessment in Higher Education* (San Francisco: Jossey-Bass, 2004). Starting with the one hundred dimensions of character identified by Wintley and his team, the professors developed this measurement instrument over the course of about six months. The assessment is designed to help individuals identify their areas of strength and weakness in the eight pillars of godly character.

Dr. Sedlacek earned his bachelor's and master's degrees from Iowa State University and his PhD from Kansas State University. He has published extensively in professional journals on a wide range of topics, including racism, sexism, college admissions, advising, and employee selection.

Dr. Duffy earned his bachelor's degree from Boston College and his master's degree and PhD from the University of Maryland. He teaches a class on positive psychology and is an expert in the psychological literature on character strengths.

Access the Your Best Destiny Personal Assessment Tool

Your complimentary access code can be found in this book
Hardcover edition: On the underside of the dust jacket
Softcover edition: Inside back cover

Visit www.YourBestDestinyAssessment.com and enter your unique code. Take the survey to determine your areas of strength. In addition to the assessment, you'll find additional resources to help you grow in each of the eight pillars.